# Kundalini

*Ultimate Guide to Awaken Your Third Eye Chakra, Develop Awareness and Spiritual Power Through Kundalini and Chakra Awakening*

**Laura Connelly**

© Copyright 2020 by Laura Connelly. All rights reserved.

The work contained herein has been produced with the intent to provide relevant knowledge and information on the topic on the topic described in the title for entertainment purposes only. While the author has gone to every extent to furnish up to date and true information, no claims can be made as to its accuracy or validity as the author has made no claims to be an expert on this topic. Notwithstanding, the reader is asked to do their own research and consult any subject matter experts they deem necessary to ensure the quality and accuracy of the material presented herein.

This statement is legally binding as deemed by the Committee of Publishers Association and the American Bar Association for the territory of the United States. Other jurisdictions may apply their own legal statutes. Any reproduction, transmission or copying of this material contained in this work without the express written consent of the copyright holder shall be deemed as a copyright violation as per the current legislation in force on the date of publishing and subsequent time thereafter. All additional works derived from this material may be claimed by the holder of this copyright.

The data, depictions, events, descriptions and all other information forthwith are considered to be true, fair and accurate unless the work is expressly described as a work of fiction. Regardless of the nature of this work, the Publisher is exempt from any responsibility of actions taken by the reader in conjunction with this work. The Publisher acknowledges that the reader acts of their own accord and releases the author and Publisher of any responsibility for the observance of tips, advice, counsel, strategies and techniques that may be offered in this volume.

# TABLE OF CONTENTS

Introduction ............................................................................................................... 1

Chapter 1 *The Third Eye Chakra* ........................................................................ 2

Chapter 2 *The Third Eye And Psychic Abilities* ............................................... 7

Chapter 3 *Exploring The Spirit World* ............................................................. 16

Chapter 4 *Seeing Other Worlds Through The Third Eye* .............................. 25

Chapter 5 *Opening Your Third Eye Chakra* ................................................... 34

Chapter 6 *The Pineal Gland And The Third Eye* ........................................... 49

Chapter 7 *Reiki Healing And The Third Eye* .................................................. 55

Chapter 8 *Psychic Abilities And Your Third Eye* ............................................ 57

Conclusion ............................................................................................................. 75

Description ............................................................................................................ 76

# INTRODUCTION

Congratulations on purchasing *Kundalini,* and thank you for doing so.

The following chapters will discuss your Third Eye chakra and the immense meaning and ability it will bring to your life when it is fully opened and functioning correctly. Your mind and soul will flood with light and love from the Universe. The world around you will become brighter and more intense than ever before. You will find yourself filled with the knowledge of all things and all of the power that the Universe will bring to you in your daily life.

Your sixth sense is present in your Third Eye chakra, and it holds your ability to see all the mysteries of the world and to live in harmony with the Universe. You will know things you have missed before and feel feelings you never knew were possible. Having fully opened this chakra is vital to your ability to use your intuition to see through the drama and illusion that may cloud your world at times. It will allow you to navigate your life on your terms, no longer being dependent on half-truths and imagery when you seek reality.

And having the Third Eye chakra fully functional will allow you to travel to other planes and communicate with the beings who reside there. The wealth of the entire Universe will be yours to sample and enjoy as your conscious mind receives messages from the Divine and other sources of spirituality.

There are plenty of books on this subject on the market, thanks again for choosing this one! Every effort has been made to ensure it is full of as much useful information as possible, please enjoy!

# CHAPTER 1
*The Third Eye Chakra*

Inside your body, placed along or near your spine from your tailbone to the top of your head, are your seven internal chakras. Your Third Eye Chakra is in the center of your forehead, between your physical eyes. Your body will communicate on a subtle level with all of the energies around you. Certain of these energies will directly relate to a specific part of your body. Of the seven internal chakras, the sixth in line is the Third Eye chakra. It directly correlates to your psychological abilities, mental skills, and how you evaluate your attitudes and beliefs. This chakra is connected directly to your pineal gland, pituitary gland, and your brain. This chakra is linked to your mind. It is responsible for your unconscious and conscious psychological tendencies as it resonates with the energy of your psyche. It is the chakra that houses your sixth sense, wisdom, and intuition.

## Location and Function of the Third Eye Chakra

Everyone has a Third Eye chakra, and everyone can open and access their Third Eye chakra if they choose to do so. You might be using it without even knowing that you are. Whenever you get that little feeling that something isn't quite right with a person or a situation, when your gut tells you something you find difficult to ignore, then that is your sixth sense in action. Your Third Eye is giving you the perceptions it has collected so that you may act upon this knowledge. Even if you are not immediately able to locate the source of this information, it is still valid and should not be ignored.

The Third Eye chakra is challenged by the need to discriminate between the source of your thoughts and feelings, and whether these are motivated by illusion, fear, or strength. You will need to develop a mind that is impersonal and find the ability to detach yourself from mental and physical illusions. To be able to know what is in your soul, you will need to transcend your thoughts, fears, and worries. Your Third Eye chakra will drive all of these functions. It holds a combination of memories, personal experiences, fears, and facts that are all unique to you and your experiences. All of these are continually active in the energy of your subtle body, which is also known as your soul.

The foundation of all the wisdom you will ever possess lives in your Third Eye chakra. It deciphers the difference between what is true and what you believe to be true in any situation. Negative memories can manifest within your mind and become truths in your later life. If an adult told your child self that you were stupid, your adult self would most likely believe that you are a foolish person. This example is just one example of a feeling that is valid to you, even though you can't produce the facts to support your theory. Your Third Eye is another sense organ that can be improved with work, and one of the things that it will do is help you dig through your opinions to find the facts behind them. It will also help you receive the vibrations that other people put off, and this will help to enhance your perceptions of life as you learn to choose who to be with and who to put aside. The person who made you feel stupid by calling you stupid might be one of those you would set aside, or at least you will know how to deal with them in the future.

Your Third Eye chakra finds its basis in truth. Many of the ideas that you currently think of as truths are nothing more than the remnants of prior negative experience, like being told you are stupid. Once you have opened your Third Eye and can see the real truth, then you will be able to rid yourself of these incorrect preconceived notions. This chakra wants to break down the stereotypical ideas you are holding on to. The world feeds you illusions, and you will be able to detach yourself from them. Your freedom will allow you to think freely and control your thoughts. There will be no limitations that you will not be able to conquer when this chakra is opened.

You will learn that there is no one person or group of people in society that will have the power to determine the path that you will walk. A larger karmic entity will now drive your life and your decisions. Until you can use the full energy of your Third Eye chakra, you might believe that the findings and opinions of other people are the keys that drive your actions, but this is just a psychic illusion meant to hold you as a captive in situations that are not healthy for you. Currently, you create karmic manifestations that cause you to suffer from illnesses or feel pain in your life. The opening of your Third Eye will help you move beyond all of that.

# Psychic Abilities

Not everyone knows how to use their psychic abilities, especially in adulthood, although everyone is born with the knowledge. Children see and feel everything because they have not yet learned that there needs to be limitations on what they can see, hear, and touch. Once children turn into adults, they usually lose the ability to tap into their psychic powers because their minds have become closed and jaded. Life's experiences have taught adults to mistrust their own better judgment, to the point that they are barely able to function on their own in the real world.

People who use their psychic abilities daily are no different from you; they have just learned how to have an intuition that goes beyond the boundaries that outline the physical world; they can taste, sense, feel, hear, and see things that most people are unable to perceive. Most people have what is deemed to be the normal perception by the guidelines of society. For most people in most situations, the perception of reality is a factual matter. You can tell when someone is not feeling well physically, and you will agree with most people that the sky is blue with white fluffy clouds. When you begin to expand your sensory abilities, you will find out that most people do not use many of the senses that are available to be used. You will become more aware of your inherently unique psychic gifts when you come to this awareness.

Psychic skills are the ability to process the sensory data that comes from both intangible and tangible sources. You will find yourself able to process this data on an intense spiritual, physical, or emotional level. This is a broad definition because psychic gifts tend to vary significantly in their application and intensity. You will enjoy a sense of oneness with the Universe when you open your Third Eye chakra and use it regularly. The main focus of many of the spiritual practices is achieving this oneness because then you will have unlocked the powers of your Third Eye and your psychic abilities.

# Telepathic Awareness

When your Third Eye chakra is open, you will be able to receive thoughts or feelings from another person over distances, and this is known as telepathy. Using telepathy does not involve using the basic five senses of sound, sight, touch, smell, or taste. With ESP, you know something without having direct contact with it. Everyone is born with the ability to be telepathic, just like everyone is born with the power of psychic abilities, but it takes conscious effort to keep these skills in use. Many people are not able to learn to use their telepathic powers because they view telepathy with mistrust and skepticism, and this keeps them from being fully able to develop their talents.

You must be well relaxed when you are trying to use your telepathic abilities to communicate with others. Your mind will need to be open and receptive to receiving information. If you continue practicing your skills at receiving messages from others and sending messages out to other people, you will eventually be able to do it with minimal effort. Envision the recipient standing with you and having a regular conversation, and use words and phrases that show great detail. Keep trying to send out your message until you feel that it has been received. As you practice more, you will become familiar with this feeling, and you will know when your intended recipient has gotten the message you are sending. When you first begin receiving notifications, they may appear as sudden thoughts, and you might be tempted to ignore them. Listen to these messages, even if you don't act on them, because this is the beginning of the lines of telepathic communication opening for you. News will come to you in various ways. You might receive feelings, thoughts, images, emotions, and desires, and these are all normal and indicate that the other person is sending messages that are full of great detail. Sometimes people can receive notices when they are asleep.

When you begin using your powers of telepathy to send and receive messages to other people, you will start to communicate with other people on a deeper and more meaningful level. You will find you have a greater understanding of others. And this form of communication will work anywhere and anytime, in any situation, so it makes sense for you to develop this ability. When you become more assertive in your practice, you will even learn how to block those people from whom you don't want to receive any messages.

The human brain is hardwired to be able to pick up subtle cues and messages from other people, although most people never use these abilities. Your mind can also send out your emotions and intentions to other people. Some people are more capable of using the power of the Third Eye chakra simply because they want to; they practice regularly and honestly believe in what they are doing. Your Third Eye chakra is the seat of all of your wisdom and knowledge and your link to the Universe. The light of the Universe is the element of the Third Eye, and its theme is the desire to see and to know all that is possible to know.

# CHAPTER 2
*The Third Eye And Psychic Abilities*

Inside your physical body is your subtle body, the spiritual part of you that receives messages from the Universe and sends messages back out. Your Third Eye chakra is what is responsible for your imagination, clairvoyance, concentration, intuition, and psychic abilities. To receive the energies of the Universe, you will need to open your Third Eye and be fully connected to it. This chakra is at the very center of your sixth sense and the source of all of your psychic powers.

Your sixth sense is the intuition that allows you to read the future as well as the past and the present. It will enable you to receive non-verbal messages from the other side of the veil, that cosmic covering that separates the living world from the world of the non-living. You will receive messages from loved ones who have gone on before you, angels, and spirit guides. You will also use your Third Eye when there is an intention that you want to manifest in your life. A purpose is an idea or a desire, and displaying merely means to make it a reality in your life. Your intention might be to lose twenty pounds, and the manifestation is when you take steps to lose that twenty pounds. You will use your Third Eye to visualize your intention, to see it as being part of reality.

Except for the Heart Chakra, which is the center chakra and the balance between the lower three and the upper three chakras, the chakras all have balancing chakras in your subtle body. The balancing chakra for the Third Eye is the Solar Plexus chakra, the center of your gut feelings. When these two chakras are opened and balanced, they will work together to enable you to cruise freely and smoothly through your life. You will still encounter difficult times and other obstacles along the way, but these are just the steps in your personal and spiritual growth. Even when you experience difficulties, you will be able to learn from them quickly and grow and move on, without finding yourself stuck in that particular situation for very long. When this chakra is open, it will give you the power to have a strong intuition, spiritual focus, and mental clarity.

# ESP (Extra Sensory Perception)

This ability allows you to receive information with your mind. This will include the capabilities of telepathy, intuition, psychometry, clairvoyance, precognition, and retrocognition. There is also the ability that is known as the second sight, where you might learn things that are not readily available to your five senses; you might receive knowledge through a vision or a dream state. ESP is your sixth sense, the power of your Third Eye. You will feel information in your gut as well as in your soul and your heart when you are receiving information using ESP. This form of psychic power, like the others, has no boundaries of time or space. You might be able to manipulate physical objects, see into the future, and know the thoughts of other people. You may experience ESP in many different ways.

Precognition – This is the ability to see into the future direction so that you will know people, places, and events before they ever happen.

Retrocognition – This is the complete opposite of precognition, because it allows you to see into the past, and especially into the distant past. You will be able to recognize past events and people that you were not part of in real-time.

Déjà vu – This involves feeling like the recent experience that you are having is an experience that you have taken part in before. With this type of ESP, you will know the details of events you should not be able to understand.

Telepathy – This is the power that allows you to know the thoughts of other people. This ability can be used to communicate with others without ever writing or speaking.

Telekinesis – This is the power to physically affect an object by using the capabilities of your mind, without ever touching the object.

Mediumship – This is the one ability that most people refuse to use because it involves communicating with deceased entities. Mediums channel the energy of the departed and receive messages from them, and then they relay those messages to the people who are waiting here in the world of the living.

# Relaxation and Emptying the Mind

The idea of emptiness is another way to look at an experience that you are having, a different way to perceive matters to help you understand them. Emptiness will not subtract from or add to the actual raw data of the experience. It will allow you to use your mind and your senses to make conclusions without wondering if there is any backstory or confidential information. This type of thinking is called emptiness because it has none of the suggestions that people usually add to an experience to try and make sense of the experience. It enables you to see the world as it is and to make sense of the events of the world that you live. People will often create mythical stories to try to explain an event or experience that they do not understand, but emptiness will eliminate that habit. When you create a view of the world to describe an adventure, you interfere with the knowledge and your ability to understand it and resolve it, because your attention is drawn away from the critical information that you need.

When you adopt the practice of relaxing and emptying your mind, then you will be able to view an experience or an event without reacting to it. You will watch the event as it happens, and you will feel no emotions in what you are seeing. You will merely try to determine what the event means in your life if it has any meaning at all. Not all of life's experiences and events will have a sense in your life, and emptying your mind will allow you to determine which experiences warrant further attention from you. You will see the truth in the event without feeling emotions.

It will take you time and practice to master the art of emptying your mind and learning to relax. The first instinct of most humans, when they face a new experience or event, is to react to the situation immediately. You will need to learn how to remove yourself from reaction and concentrate on viewing what is happening. Spend some time every day; focus on the ideas and perceptions that you hold as truths. See which of your thoughts you can get rid of, because this will help you empty your mind, and a clear mind is a relaxed mind. Lose your preconceived notions and assumptions about your views and stories. Removing these from your mind will remove suffering and stress since it will be eliminating anger, greed, and delusions. Your mind will be clear, free from the garbage that is limiting your psychic abilities.

# Parallel Worlds

When you have activated your Third Eye chakra and your psychic powers are healthy, you will be able to interact with entities in parallel worlds. These worlds do exist, and those entities already interact with people on Earth. There is important evidence that points to the existence of parallel worlds. In the world of quantum physics, it is suggested that every possible outcome of a particular situation will happen. Still, they will all happen on different planes and in other Universes. Only one conclusion can occur in each Universe. To allow this theory to be a reality, there would need to be as many parallel worlds as there are possible outcomes to a situation. There is also the idea of the multiverse in physics. If we believe that our Universe began with the Big Bang, then it is possible to think that many other Universes started with a similar Big Bang. While some people say there is no concrete evidence that other worlds exist, there is also no substantial evidence that proves they do not exist.

In the center of your physical brain, there is a small gland, about the shape and size of a small pine cone that is known as the pineal gland. Ancient teachers believed that the pineal gland was surrounded by a substance that was much like vapor and was the point of entry into the soul of the human. We know now that the pineal gland is part of your endocrine system, and its job is to secrete the hormone melatonin, the hormone that is responsible for controlling your circadian rhythms, those regular cycles of sleeping and being awake that is ruled by the presence or absence of light and dark. The pineal gland does not produce melatonin when there is discernible light, so people sleep at night and stay awake in the daytime. The melatonin that the pineal gland secretes is the hormone that induces sleep.

Mystics and seers once revered the pineal gland because they believed that it had some control over the Third Eye chakra. Since they saw that light and dark guided the human in their sleeping and waking, and since they knew that all entry into the human soul came through the vapor surrounding the pineal gland, they believed that the pineal gland was somehow involved with bringing information from outside the mind to the soul inside of the body. The pineal gland is a sensor that specializes in detecting the changes outside your body and makes the necessary internal changes to make physiological adjustments. The pineal gland gives you the feeling of well-being when it works harmoniously with your Third Eye so that you feel a heightened tendency toward spirituality. Your Third Eye attaches you to your subtle body, as it is the bridge between the spirit world and you. Your Third Eye will see the reality that is beyond what your human eyes see, especially in matters relating to entities in parallel worlds. The doorway to all psychic and spiritual values will be open to you, and you will be able to use lucid dreaming, telepathy, clairvoyance, and astral projection as you wish.

## Astral Mind Travel

Depending on the tradition that it is referring to, astral mind travel can go by many different names. Whether it is known by one of the western terms of dream body, celestial body, or energy body; or the diamond body of Taoism, the Egyptian ka, the Buddhist light body, the subtle body of Tantric tradition, the Hindu body of bliss, or the Christian experience of the different heavens, it is all a form of astral mind travel. The human body includes the physical structure and the subtle body, and it is your subtle body that is active while you are dreaming and is responsible for projecting astrally. Your out-of-body experiences are the combination of your dreams and astral projection. When your subtle body is well cultivated, then it will be able to survive the physical body as a model for consciousness.

Astral mind travel is also known as an out-of-body experience or OOBE. These can be intentional, or they can happen involuntarily while you are sleeping. You can also trigger an OOBE by depriving yourself of water and food, or if you are sick or you suffer from some physical or mental trauma. Lucid dreams make excellent opportunities for astral mind travel. You begin the experience by observing your sleeping form after you have left your body. Practice will allow you to be able to direct your awareness to particular locations or activities. Your subtle body is the area of your form that will do the traveling. Your rational mind and your physical body are linked to one another by your subtle body, the intermediate body of light that travels the astral planes. When your celestial body is having an OOBE, it is crossing the astral planes of other Universes.

Astral travel also validates the existence of life after the death of the physical body. When you have experience with astral travel, you will be completely aware of yourself outside of your physical body. You will be able to touch, hear, smell, see, and taste from the area around you. When you are deeply in meditation, soundly sleeping, or engaging in conscious astral travel, a switch is activated that allows you to travel on other planes. This switch is the activation of the pineal gland, which releases chemicals that cause your subtle body to leave your physical body, whether you are consciously traveling astrally, deep into your meditation, having a lucid dream, or at the point of death. And having your Third Eye chakra open and healthy is necessary for all of this to happen.

Since your subconscious is in control of your soul while you are sleeping, you have no amount of control over what happens unless you have a lucid dream. If you are doing so, then you can have a heavenly mind experience and travel out of your body. There are some benefits for you to practice astral mind travel consciously. You will be able to travel well beyond the boundaries of the physical world and its rational thought processes. Your inner spiritual being will blossom, and you will experience a definite boost in your astral abilities. You can enjoy a complete transformation of your perspective of yourself as a spiritual and physical being in this world. You might find that you will operate with a greater sense of consciousness in the daily activities of your life after you experience astral mind travel. The reason for this is that you are now secure in the knowledge that you are more than just a mere physical being who is doomed to live a boring life and be forgotten after death.

It is reasonably simple to prepare your body to have a heavenly mind travel experience. This is often best done in the early hours of the morning because it is easier for you to reach the relaxed state of being and heightened awareness that is needed. This can also be done just before you fall asleep for the night. Astral mind travel is a personal experience, so have your experience when the time is right for you. Do this when you get into bed since your physical body will need to be completely relaxed. And since astral mind travel is a personal experience, it is best to prepare for it when you are alone. Keep the room dark and silent and get rid of anything that might distract you.

Lie flat on your back and clear your mind. The goal is for you to reach a state where your mind and body are completely relaxed. Breathe in and out, slowly and evenly. Try not to think of anything, either thought about your day or thoughts about the travel you are about to take. If you have a crystal to clear your Third Eye chakra, you can place it on your forehead while you are relaxing. Let your physical body, and your subtle body get close to the edge of sleep, but do not allow yourself to fall asleep just yet. For astral mind travel to occur, you will need to be at that thin line between being awake and being asleep. Keep your eyes completely closed, and your focus on one part of your body. Try to make that part move by using only the power of your mind. Keep broadening your focus until you have included your entire body in your direction. Continue until you can proceed forward with your whole body by using the power of your mind.

Now it is vitally important, more than ever before, for you to remain relaxed because you will likely feel a series of movements like little waves as your soul gets ready to leave your body. If you feel any fear at this moment, your soul will not go and you will not be able to engage in astral mind travel. Let the vibrations of the waves carry you while you continue to remain relaxed and peaceful. Use the power of your mind once again to move your body to a standing position. As you stand up, take a look around the room that your physical body is lying in, then walk across the room and turn and look at yourself, all while using just the powers of your mind. If your physical body can feel you looking at yourself from across the room, then your experiment was successful, and you are ready for astral mind travel.

You might want some concrete proof that you are engaged in astral mind travel. Go into another room and move an object, looking at it closely before you set it back down. Then when you awaken, you can physically go into the other room and find that object. When you have completely mastered this technique, then you have mastered astral mind travel. Eventually, you will want to travel to new locations that are not as familiar to you. When you travel, always try to mentally record details of the places where you go, so that you can go back and look for these places later. When you use astral mind travel to go to unfamiliar places, they will seem familiar when your physical body goes there. Astral mind travel is perfectly safe, and you will always return to where you came from.

## Controlling your Dreams

You might have already experienced a lucid dream. If you have ever been dreaming, and then suddenly you told yourself that this is a dream because you were sure that you were dreaming, then that is a lucid dream. If you have ever controlled the storyline that the dream had, then that is also a lucid dream. Most people dream all of the time and never know that they are dreaming until they wake up and recall parts of the dream. Lucid dreams happen during periods of rapid eye movement, just like all other dreams do.

Lucid dreams usually happen spontaneously, although it is possible to train yourself to have a lucid dream. The ability of people to control their dreams varies widely. Lucid dreaming is a process that will let you explore the worlds that are inside your mind even while you are entirely aware that you are dreaming. There are many practical applications for the use of lucid dreaming in real-world situations. One way to use lucid dreaming is for people who have recurring nightmares to grab control of the nightmare and change its course consciously. You are less likely to be afraid of something that you can control. You can also use lucid dreaming as a form of entertainment because it will allow you to travel anywhere and do anything that you want.

There are things that you can do if you want to practice lucid dreaming. One method of testing your dreaming is called reality testing. This will help you to verify whether or not you are in a dream. While you are dreaming, check the time on a clock, and recheck it several minutes later. If you have a lucid dream, the time will fluctuate wildly, not go at a natural pace as it does when you are awake. For your dream to be considered a lucid dream, it will need to have four common characteristics. You will need to know that you are dreaming, the things you see in your dream might disappear when you wake up, your dream will not follow any standard rules of physical laws, and you know that there is another world that is outside of the dream world that you are in. The dream does not need to make sense; you just need to be able to understand what is going on in the dream. For example, if you dream that you can flap your arms and fly through the air and it makes sense to you in the dream, then you have a lucid dream. It doesn't matter that people really can't fly, since the physical laws of the real world do not apply in the lucid dream.

Lucid dreams work in four stages, each one being more profound than the step before. The first level is the normal level of non-lucid dreaming, where most people begin. When you are in this state, you will have no idea that you are dreaming and anything that you see, you will recall later and accept it as being part of reality. You will not have any conscious control of your dream, and it will be entirely created from your mind. In the second level, you will begin dreaming of something that seems impossible in the middle of dreaming about something possible. Your unconscious mind is being blocked by something in your conscious mind, so while you might want to leave the dream, you are not able to. At this point, you are partially aware that you are dreaming and somewhat not. When you reach the third level of lucid dreaming, you will be able to have an utterly lucid dream as long as you are willing to accept the lucid dream. You need to realize that you are in a dream and be ready to stay there and experience the dream. The most important part of the lucid dream is not in control of the dream, but in being willing to play along with the dream. On the fourth level, you will be able to experience the end of the dream, whether it comes to a conclusion or ends, and you will wake up.

Developing your Third Eye is your doorway to all possible psychic experiences you could have. When this ability is cultivated, then the separation between spirit and self will dissolve. You will feel cynicism, jealousy, uncertainty, pessimism, and confusion if this chakra is blocked. The highest source of divine energy will come through an open Third Eye. Opening this chakra will bring you the ability to engage in astral projection and lucid dreaming. This will also give you an enhanced imagination and a better quality of sleep.

# CHAPTER 3
*Exploring The Spirit World*

The spirit world is that realm that is inhabited by spirits, those spiritual manifestations that inhabit other parallel worlds. This external environment for souls is independent of the natural world that you settle, but the natural world and the spirit world are continually interacting with one another. These two worlds continuously communicate with each other through various methods.

There are many realms of existence beyond the physical world in which you live. The domains operate on different vibrational frequencies than this one because each part is on a different level of energy. When you travel between the realms, you will become aware of a change, a shift in the power from one kingdom to another. The spirit realms also do not operate like the physical realm in which you live, where many different people make a melting pot of humans and their characteristics. In the spirit world, each domain is the location of spirits who have achieved a particular level in their spirituality. When people leave this physical realm, they do not immediately become saints or angels. People who pass on will retain their personality and memory, and they will continue in much the same form as they did when they were alive, but in one of the spirit realms.

When you leave this physical world, you will go to the realm that you deserve to go to, a plan which is based on how you lived your life in this realm. This level of spirituality will be reflected in the vibration of your aura. Your vibrations will be higher if you have been a spiritual person in this realm. You will then pass into the realm that most closely matches your vibrational level. These inhabitants of these spirit realms will visit your physical realm, and they encourage communication between the domains.

## Clairvoyance

This word translates into a clear vision. Clairvoyance is the ability to learn information about a person, object, location, or event by using your psychic abilities and extra-sensory perceptions (ESP). People who use ESP are clairvoyants who use the power of clear sight to see persons or events that are in distant time or space. There are three different abilities that all fall under the umbrella of prophecy. Remote viewing is the perception of events that are currently happening that are outside of your normal range of perception, like events that happen far away. Precognition gives you the ability to know or predict future events, and retrocognition is the ability to view events that are from the past.

Clairvoyants will see things with their mind's eyes, using their sixth sense through their Third Eye chakra. The real talent of the clairvoyant is the ability to determine the meaning of a message or an image that they receive. This enables them to decipher the vibrations that other people emit as well as receive notifications from the spirit world. Many people are clairvoyant without realizing that they are, but they will display certain traits or talents. If you have mental images randomly flash into your mind, if you see visions in your mind that look like a movie is playing or if you get flashing images of numbers, colors, symbols, or other images, then you may have clairvoyant abilities. This is especially true if you see flashes of colors or bright lights, as these may be angels or spirit guides trying to communicate with you to send you a message. Since prophecy has a lot to do with seeing mental or physical images, visualization is a big part of being clairvoyant.

You might be able to assemble an object without reading the direction or repair a small appliance because you can see in your mind how the item should operate. You might never get lost because you have a marvelously innate sense of direction. You excel at assembling puzzles, completing mazes, and reading maps because the tasks that require visual traits and spatial abilities are your specialty. You prefer jobs that allow you to use your sense of creativity, and you dearly love beautiful things. Your dreams are often really vivid due to your overactive imagination. If you have some of these traits, or even if you don't but would like to develop them, then you can do some or all of the following exercises.

Meditation – The practice of meditation is essential to being a clairvoyant and to opening your Third Eye chakra. When you practice your meditation regularly, you will develop your psychic gifts and improve the vision of your Third Eye. You will be able to clear your senses, raise your vibration, and get out of your logical mind.

Keep a Dream Journal – Clairvoyants will usually have vivid dreams, and writing them down in a notebook is an excellent way to develop your abilities. When your logical mind is at rest, your subconscious mind takes over, so that it is free to receive messages from the spirit world. Sleep time can be a great time to play when your subconscious mind is making connections with the spirit world and engaging in astral travel. It is a good idea for you to keep your dream journal right beside your bed. This will allow you to write down your dreams the moment you wake up while they are still fresh in your mind. You can also plan to receive messages from the spirits by merely setting an intention while you are falling asleep.

Playing with Crystals – Crystals are invaluable to anyone who is working with their chakras, their aura, or developing their psychic abilities. Use a crystal to open your Third eye, and to keep it open and healthy. Put a crystal on a table near you while you are meditating, or hold it in your hand gently. Put the crystal on the table next to your bed when you sleep. While clear quartz will work on any chakra, a piece of amethyst or fluorite is both renowned for their ability to heal your Third Eye chakra. Other good choices for crystal therapy for the Third Eye chakra are aquamarine, opal, emerald, and celestite.

Play Games that Encourage Clairvoyance – Simple games will help you strengthen your clairvoyant abilities while you are having fun playing them. Play the card game 'memory.' To play this game, you will lay all of a deck of cards face down, and then you will turn them over two at a time, looking for pairs of the same card. Have a family member or friend set a group of ten unrelated items on a table. Study the things for one minute, and then leave the room. While you are gone, the other person will remove one of the items and hide it out of your view. When you return to the room, you will need to tell which item is missing.

Practice Visualization – the Clairvoyants, will need to have strong abilities for visualization, so this is one trait that you will need to practice. Clairvoyants see with their mind's eye, their Third Eye, so all of the visions, pictures, and symbols that you see will be in your mind. You will find it much easier to receive images if your Third Eye is open and functioning correctly. Take some time every day to visualize different photos, scenes, and pictures in your mind. Relax while you are doing this and try to have fun with it, using images to create images in your mind.

# Premonitions

Spirituality is based on the awareness that you are connected to something greater than yourself or your ego. This something greater goes by many different names, depending on the beliefs of the particular person. Religious people might refer to the higher power as the Almighty, God, Yahweh, Buddha, or Allah. Those who are not believers in one formal religion but consider themselves spiritual creatures might refer to the Great Spirit, the Absolute, or the power in the Universe. And some people don't refer to any name at all but prefer to think of the higher power as a sense of infinite beauty and fantastic order. Whether you label it or not, that something greater provides you with a sense of meaning and strength in your life.

As people mature spiritually, they will often find that their power of knowing and seeing expands. These elevated abilities often include the capacity to understand events that have not yet happened, events that are in the future. There is a long line of seers, shamans, visionaries, and prophets that will attest to this possibility. The modern version of this ability is now known as the sixth sense, gut feelings, intuition, or hunches.

Premonitions have a deep connection to spirituality, especially when the suspicion involves someone we love or care deeply about. Premonitions will open you up to other people and the rest of the Universe. They show that you are part of something much larger than yourself, that you are an element in the fabric that connects all the beings in your Universe. Premonitions reveal the oneness that exists when minds are linked across time and space. They are proof that you are not an isolated individual, but a person whose individual consciousness operates outside beyond your physical body. They suggest that you are infinite in time and space. Premonitions are the window through which you can see your connection to the Divine.

You can test your hunches to determine whether or not your suspicions are real. Before you know who is calling on the phone, try to guess who the caller is. Try to imagine what a store will look like on the inside while you are still outside of the door. The ability to know these things is not luck; it is premonition. When you experience déjà vu, do not be afraid of it because there is nothing scary about it. Déjà vu is merely telling you that you have knowledge of this place or person before you are physically there, and that is a premonition. People often ignore that nagging feeling in their gut, but you should not, because that is just a suspicion that something about this person or situation is not right.

Many people will experience their premonitions while they are dreaming. They can see the people who are involved in the situation and the situation itself. This is known as having a premonitory dream. Your mind is showing you something that will happen in the future in real life. If you can have this kind of vision, then you can be susceptible to events that are not easily explained in simple terms. You are probably more intuitive and open-minded than most people you know. The most significant difference between regular dreams and premonitory dreams is that premonitory dreams are based on real situations. You will find yourself in a situation watching people do things, and it could be part of a dream, and it could be happening in real life. In a vision, the events of the dream are created from your mind, and you are in control of the events of the dream. When you have a premonitory dream, the events of the dream will come to you, and you will merely watch them unfold, as though you were watching a movie on a screen. You will have no control over the dream. And these are easy to recall when you wake up because premonitory dreams are informative and very vivid.

There is a definite reason for your sixth sense being activated, as it is in a premonitory dream. The dream is trying to give you information so that you will be aware of a coming situation and you will know what to do when you encounter it. When you sleep, your mind is free from the restraints of the physical world, and it is open to go in whichever direction it chooses to go. If a particular premonitory dream keeps returning to you, it is best if you pay attention, because your spirit guide is trying to tell you something.

## Daydreams

The act of daydreaming is allowing a steady stream of conscious thoughts to keep you from doing those things you are supposed to be doing, or it might merely be a way to pass the time pleasantly. It will direct your attention inward to personal and internal matters and away from the external issues that are surrounding you. Almost everyone daydreams, and no two imaginations are ever identical in content. Fantasies serve to assist you with thinking about the future, thinking creatively, and thinking of new ways to deal with old issues, refreshing your attention span, and thinking creatively.

Daydreaming is an excellent release from boredom. Daydreaming will allow you to let your thoughts wander during those times when you are engaged in some tedious task, or you are somewhere you would rather not be. Sometimes the stimulus coming in from outside is repetitive and causes you to tune it out with daydreaming. This lets you relieve the strain on your mind by mentally stepping away from the repetitive information so that you can return to it when you want to. If you are facing several different problems at the same time, you might want to daydream about different outcomes for the situations. This will allow you to switch your thoughts between other streams of information if you have several goals you need to plan for. Creativity is increased in people who daydream, especially in those people who daydream while they are trying to solve a complicated problem. When you use daydreaming about speculating about future events, you will have the opportunity to plan your reaction to them and their possible conclusions. This will also help you keep your mind off your goals while you try to plot the course of action that is the best for you to reach them.

Man has long been interested in the workings and wanderings of the human mind. Your brain comes with a built-in default network since it is made up of specific structures, and all human brains are built the same. The system in your mind will link several areas together to create sensory experiences. These experiences cause the brain to think about things that are apart from the events that are entering the mind from sources outside of the brain. Daydreams and fantasies are other words for the unique workings and wanderings of your mind.

Daydreams are not just useful tools to keep you from being bored, but they have practical purposes of serving. They allow you to explore your inner thoughts and ideas. Daydreams are particularly useful when you are trying to contemplate your past experiences, creating images of events you hope will happen to you in the future, trying to decipher the thoughts or actions of other people, or if you are faced with an ethical or moral decision. The default network in your brain makes your daydreams possible, and the nature of the dreams will have a direct effect on your soul and your mind. People often daydream about something they want but do not have, such as a partner or a better job. You can use your daydreaming time to help yourself in various ways.

Turn off the default network in your brain when you need to focus on something, and allow your mind to daydream. You will learn new skills or concepts better and faster if you daydream a bit while you are learning. Use your daydreams to write a unique life story for yourself, especially if something about your actual life is unsatisfying to you. Daydream about your current situation and create ways to make it better. You will perform better in your daily activities if you daydream about things that are familiar to you and not try to create new worlds for your mind to explore. And don't spend so much time daydreaming that it causes you to neglect your daily duties, but do allow yourself to daydream daily.

You will reveal much about your personality based on the details of your daydream. You are self-reflecting when you replay or rehearse your actions or thoughts during your fantasies. If your dreams are filled with negative thoughts about your life, then you might become mired in self-pity. Use your daydreaming to rewrite your experiences and make yourself the winner of every situation, as this will help you in your real-world life with others.

## Your Personal Spirit Guide

There is an entity whose job is to help you, protect you, and guide you through your life. This is your spirit guide, and when your Third Eye is fully opened, then you will be able to find your spirit guide and communicate with them. This guide might be an ancestor who has gone on before you, an angel, or only a being of another astral plane which has been given the job of watching over you. They might have been with you in another life and need to continue until their job is completed satisfactorily. While you will have some sort of close relationship with your guide, communication is entirely up to you. The spirit guide is not allowed to make the first contact, but they can reach out to you after you initiate contact with them. They will guide you silently until then unless you are in great danger when they must step in to help you.

You need to fully believe in your spirit guide if you want to contact them. Most people will have more than one spirit guide. You are born with the one who will remain with you until you die, but sometimes other spirit guides are assigned to you for particular reasons. If there exists the need, you can always ask for more spirit guides to come to you. All of your spirit guides will work together for the common good of you. There are helper angels whose job is to wander the Universe in search of people who need them the most at any particular time. The Ascended Masters were once humans who passed on into the next realm and became leaders in the world of spirits. They will work to keep you safe and to guide your development in all things spiritual. You will have one Guardian Angel, and that is the angel that was assigned to you when you were born, who will remain with you until you die. The archangels are the assistants of the Ascended Masters, and they are also leaders in the spirit world. Archangels usually have one area of expertise they try to assist with. And sometimes one of your spirit guides will be your spirit animal, the spiritual embodiment of one of your beloved pets who has crossed the rainbow bridge. Your spirit guides will not contact you directly, but they will send you messages, like a dream to help you solve a nagging problem or a song that has special meaning to you. You can use different methods to communicate with your spirit guide once your Third Eye is entirely open:

- Improve your intuition
- Develop a spiritual practice of your own
- Use methods of divination like runes or tarot cards
- Daydream about your spirit guide
- Give a problem to them to help you solve
- Give them their unusual name
- Write to them in a journal
- Never stop looking for signs that they are with you

## Mediums and Channeling

Of all of the forms of communicating with the spirit world, this is the one that is most often misunderstood and most often avoided. The medium connects with the spirit to speak, and the medium will be able to exert some level of control over the soul and how they act and what they say. Mediums do communicate with the deceased, and this is the part that bothers many people, but the spirits that are helping you are the spirits of dead people. How the medium and the soul will interact will depend significantly on the abilities of the medium, the intent of the communication, and the conditions the communication is taking place under.

When a spirit is allowed to control the medium, the medium enters a state of trance. The soul will then communicate through the medium instead of the medium, relaying the words and thoughts of the spirit to the person or people who called for contact with the soul. The medium at work is nothing more than a human instrument to allow the spirit to speak, a channel that the words of the soul can come through. The medium can help the spirit bring a particular message to the listeners. The soul is on the astral plane, and the medium is on an earthly plane, and the two beings communicate with one another.

Your physical eyes will show you what you need to see in the world around you, but your Third Eye will open up all of the possibilities of the Universe. A wide-open Third Eye will open your mind to the possibilities of life beyond the physical world. It gives you a unique sense that allows you to send and receive information at will. Your Third Eye will allow you to understand your connections with the Universe and those who live in it. And as these possibilities open up before you, will feel more powerful and more spiritual every day.

# CHAPTER 4
*Seeing Other Worlds Through The Third Eye*

The astral plane, the world of the spirits, is inhabited by the spiritual manifestations of various entities, and it is known as the otherworldly environment for souls. This world is independent of the natural world that humans inhabit, although these two worlds regularly interact with each other. The entities of both worlds can communicate with each other across the astral planes. Humans have been looking for answers for centuries about the spiritual world. Man has learned many different ways to connect with and communicate with the planets that are beyond their own to gain higher power and spiritual knowledge.

## The Art of Divination

The ability to foretell foresees, predict, or receive inspiration from the spirit world or a divine power is divination. When you practice divination, you are attempting to gain insight into a question or a situation by asking for information through a particular practice or ritual. You can make direct contact with a spirit or a god, or you can read signs, events, or omens. The method behind divination is to systematically organize all of the disjointed or random facts of the situation so that you can use them to provide you with insight into a situation or problem.

Divination has been used by oracles and seers for centuries to divine the truth from the spirit world. A prophet is a person who provides precognition or prediction using information that they received from the gods, to provide prophetic or insightful counsel to local leaders. The words of the oracle were deemed to be the words of the gods handed down for the leaders to act upon. Seers never spoke directly with gods as the prophets did, but their job was to interpret the signs the gods left for the humans. The seers used all of the methods at their disposal to obtain information, but they could not give detailed answers to the leaders as the oracles could. Through the sight of their Third Eye, they were able to provide solutions to the destiny of man. Using knowledge of past events and theories of future events, someone practicing divination can give insights into current events. When you have fully opened and engaged your Third Eye, there will be numerous methods of divination available for you to use.

Scrying has been used since ancient times, and it is one of the oldest methods of divination that is available to use. The traditional picture of a person practicing scrying is the old crone bending over her crystal ball. The word comes from words that mean 'to reveal' or 'to make out.' So the practice of scrying is all about revealing the things that are unseen by using your second sight and the power of your Third Eye. Your second sight will give you the ability to see something that can't generally be perceived by using your five senses.

Scrying will allow you to get in touch with your unconscious mind and all of the realms of your soul. It is a powerful form of analyzing yourself and understanding your intentions. Scrying is a beautiful method for getting in touch with your most personal goals, dreams, and needs if you are struggling with your purpose, meaning, or direction in life. Scrying is usually done by using some reflective surface, but there are other methods you can use for scrying. You can drip candle wax onto the water and then interpret the words or images the wax drippings form as they harden. Relax your vision and stare into a mirror, and then wait for the images to appear to you. Stare into a body of water and then read the images that you see there. Watch the flames of a roaring fire or the smoke rising from the fire for shapes and images. Gaze up at the fluffy clouds floating in the sky and see what ideas and forms are revealed to you.

When you are scrying, it is essential to be able to let your mind wander but keep your focus on the object, so it does require some amount of practice to become proficient at scrying. You need to allow your conscious mind to open and allow thoughts and feelings to flow freely through your Third Eye.

## Dreaming of Symbols

Dreams are the messages that the higher powers of the Universe send to you, and they will often hold symbols and images that will bring you a particular meaning that is relevant in the natural world. There is an infinite amount of symbols and images that can come to you in your dreams. Anything that you can dream about can bring you a more profound psychological and emotional experience and significance than the item or event itself. If you dream about a house, it can carry many different meanings. A place might symbolize somewhere that you used to live, it might be something you want to achieve in your life, or it might carry a more profound meaning tied to an event in your prior life experience, especially in your childhood. Then you might have dreams where you are exploring different houses if you want to change something in your waking life. If you are craving the simpler life you enjoyed as a child, then you might dream about your childhood home. The key to understanding what the house is trying to tell you is tied to your reaction to the house. If you are seeking change and you dream about exploring homes, then the way you react to the homes will tell you when you need to keep looking and when you have found what you are looking for. Images and symbols in dreams do not have just one meaning, but some things are so familiar to see in dreams that they have acquired meanings that are generally accepted as the message they are bringing.

- A chase scene means that you are avoiding something important in your life; you are running away from something or someone that you need to confront and resolve.
- Water is indicative of the emotional state you are currently experiencing, whether the water is calm and peaceful or wild and crashing.
- Any kind of vehicle reflects an obstacle that you need to face or the direction you want your life to go to.
- Different people and different kinds of people in your dreams are reflections of your personality traits.
- When you dream of being back in school, you are looking for lessons in the events from your childhood.
- Dreaming about being paralyzed is an indication that you feel overwhelmed by something or someone in your life, or that you feel you are tied to a specific person or situation.
- Dreaming about death is not an omen of things to come, but an indication that something in your life needs to end or go away.
- Flying in dreams is the correlation of how you feel your life is going. The way that you are flying is a direct indication of the current path of your life, so flying out of control means that you feel your life is out of control.
- Falling is scary anytime, but in your dream, it is telling you that you need to let go of something that you are hanging on to in your life.
- You might fear feeling vulnerable if you dream that you are naked in a public place.
- Dreaming about having a baby does not always mean that you want a baby; it usually means that you are looking for something new and fresh in your life.

- Food can mean so many different things in your life. It might mean you need nourishment on an emotional or spiritual level. It might mean you are seeking knowledge or energy, or new insights into the way your life is going.

## Etheric Entities

The ability to work with the entities of the etheric world is needed for your spiritual work. An entity of the etheric world is a being that is non-material and energetic. When you begin your process of awakening, you will have a great desire for new information. This new awareness will lead you through the darkness that is on the earthly plane and out the other side to the light of the other side. You will encounter the entities of the etheric as you seek for the new information that you desire. These entities will significantly differ in their form and power. Their level of energy is directly linked to their status in the spirit world.

You will have the opportunity to interact with many different types of etheric entities. You will encounter complex spirits, cultivated spirits, simple spirits, angels, disembodied humans, and deities. The many facets of the cosmos will be directly reflected in the different entities of the etheric. The larger fields of consciousness and power within the etheric realm are the deities. The various other spirits are more localized entities, and they are a smaller presence in the etheric realm. They can change their form whenever they want to. By interacting with the entities of the etheric, you will be able to draw upon a larger collective of energy and consciousness.

By opening your Third Eye, Chakra, you will begin to develop the skills that you will need to see these entities and communicate with them when you desire. To become aware of their presence, you will use your etheric perception, and when you want to share with them, you will use your etheric communication. You will be able to determine the kind of interaction that you will have with the entities of the etheric by assessing the nature of your personal goal, the type of entity that you are interacting with, and the particular relationship that you have with that entity. Your subtle body will determine the level of the relationship that you will have with the entities of the etheric. Your relationship will also depend on the particular entity that you are engaging in.

Cultivated entities are those simple creatures that were created by unique techniques to cast energy. They are also known as servitors, forms of thought, or artificial elements. When cultivated entities are sufficiently developed, they will be capable of showing the essential functions of the entities of the etheric. For reasons of practicality, they will often attach themselves to a material form. They prefer particular material forms such as paintings, clay figures, wax figures, statues, talismans, and crystals. They will infuse the material item with the essence of their spirit so that they can carry out simple tasks using elements of magic. These cultivated entities were created for the sole purpose of serving other entities, so they like to make themselves useful at all times. They are an external example of your consciousness and the force of your life as an extension of you.

Simple spirits have a limited amount of power because they are primal elementals and spirits of nature. They have almost no effect on the reality of the realm of the etheric, and they are most often encountered at the lowest levels of energy. Complex spirits have the power to affect validity. In ancient folklore, these spirits were known as elves, fairies, sprites, and demons. The complex spirits are natural allies for those who practice magic. The disembodied humans are nothing more than the souls of people who are deceased and are either unable to move on, or they refuse to move on.

The deities of the etheric world are the powerful ancient entities that human beings have been interacting with and communicating with for centuries. They are known as gods and goddesses in mythology and folklore. They exist as vast fields of complex consciousness within the etheric realm. Deities will often manifest themselves into human form because that is the form that is most easily seen by the human eye, and they need to be able to communicate with humans. You will enjoy a broader sense of consciousness and power when you can make a connection with a deity. While you are gathering strength from them, they will also be taking energy from you, along with your thoughts and emotions, because this is what gives them their power.

## Inhabitants of the Astral Planes

When celestial bodies cross over from life on earth, they go to the astral plane. This is the place that is inhabited by angels, spirits, and immature beings. The astral plane is located two full planes above the physical plane that is known as earth or the material plane of being. A heavenly spirit is a being that has been separated from their human form, although they are free to take a human form and rejoin the people of earth at any time they wish. The astral spirits usually like to take on manifestations of their kind of design. You have probably encountered a heavenly being during your time on earth and not even realized you had an encounter.

The wonderful person you encountered may have been a succubus. When you are viewing the inhabitants of the astral plane, your human eyes are not useful, since they are often taken in by what they see. A succubus is a beautiful creation that harbors a dark interior. This creature will wait for your invitation to them since they prefer to take the passive route and let you be the aggressor. Then they will present themselves as the physical manifestation of your idea of the perfect beauty. When you enter a relationship with a succubus, it will be excellent at first, but eventually, the relationship will turn dark as the succubus begins to reveal their true self, but you will not have the power to see this until you are so far involved that you feel trapped. Ask the entity directly if you want to know for sure if you are dealing with a succubus. Celestial beings have no capacity for falsehoods, and they are not able to lie to you.

You probably encountered a fairy when you were a child because children can easily see into the astral plane. All of the innocents of the world are true believers, so they enjoy an active connection to everything they encounter in this world. The etheric creatures that reside in the world of the fairies are not just happy little creatures that fly around on ethereal wings showing their beautiful colors. All of nature is the residence of the fairies, and every aspect that is found in nature is represented by a fairy. The ancient being understood the fairies and believed in them completely. Fairies will happily coexist with all of the spirits in the astral plane and all of the humans on earth.

Your spiritual progress and growth will be inhibited by an archon. The spiritual energy that radiates off of the life forms of the astral plane and the earthly plane is the food for these parasitic creatures. Archons are so evil because they are angels who have fallen from grace. They attempt to pass themselves off as sources of light and joy even though they are completely evil in nature. Archons want to infect everything and everyone with their evil intentions. They will do anything in their power to disrupt your spiritual progress.

Thought forms are the entities that represent every emotion or thought that you have ever experienced in your life. In the astral plane, those emotions and thoughts exist in the abstract form. The thought-forms in the astral plane will automatically behave with the knowledge that has been infused into them by the person they were with. All of the thought-forms that you encounter on the astral plane will fill you with greater strength and a sense of purpose. The people, places, and things that you see in your dreams are all versions of the thought-forms from the astral planes. You will often interact with your own emotions and thoughts. It is vital that you try to always remain in some control of your feelings and thoughts because thought forms will exist in both the physical world and the astral world. Your wayward thoughts and extreme emotions will cause your thought-forms to be entirely out of control.

## Seeing Into the Afterlife

Your unique stream of consciousness will continue to live on in the astral plane after you die and leave your physical body behind. This could be your subtle body, your spirit, or some part of your essence that is left behind. The beliefs that you hold when you are on the physical plane will determine the destination that your identity will take after your death. You might go on to one of the astral planes. You might begin your life again after you are born back into the world, having no conscious memory of the experience you had before. The main reason that most people fear death is that we have no idea what will happen to us next. There is no real way to know that there is life beyond the one you are living now. There are reports of people having near-death experiences where they describe the bright light, the softness, and the beautiful colors. But the tunnel at the end of all of this beauty might be nothing more than the hallway that takes you to the end of your existence with nothing beyond that to look forward to.

An atheist will have very different views regarding the end of life than someone who has some sort of religious belief. The atheist does not believe in God. Therefore they also do not believe in Heaven as a destination for life after death. Some people think there is a possibility for reincarnation or the option of continuing in some form on an astral plane. The Buddhists do not believe that the soul moves on after death but that the person themselves will be reincarnated a short time after they die. The Hindus also believe in reincarnation and the passing on of the soul. The ideal of the Christians will depend on the particular denomination that they subscribe to, but overall they believe in God as a reality and Heaven as the place that they will go after they die.

If you believe that you will move on to another plane like the astral plane after you die, then you will have the possibility of meeting the Masters. Also known as the Ascended Masters, they are the spiritually enlightened beings who have moved on from this world, leaving their earthly bodies behind for a spiritual existence. They have completed their life cycles and moved beyond the incarnations offered in the physical realm. They are now able to dwell forever in the highest of the astral planes, the Fifth Dimension. When these people were completing their last incarnation on earth, they were known as Yogi, Guru, Shaman, or Spiritual master. During their previous incarnations, they were able to learn all of the lessons that they needed to learn to move on to that exalted level. They were able to complete the divine plan that was set for them and balance out their karmic balance with enough positive to wipe out the negative they had accumulated in their lives. The Ascended Master is very close to the level of the gods. In their new incarnations, they will act as the teachers for human beings while they are working from the spirit realm. They will attend to the spiritual needs of humans by inspiring and motivating the spiritual growth of those they choose to help. Any human can eventually achieve the rank of Ascended Master by following the path of goodness and gathering positive karma throughout all of their incarnations on earth.

## Reincarnation

When a soul leaves the body of the deceased person and moves into the body of a newly born person, then that is an act of reincarnation. It is also known as a rebirth or transmigration. As a religious view of life after death, it means that the spirit or the soul of the human will start a new life in a new form after they die. The belief in reincarnation is taught as part of fact by many of the religions of the Far East like Jainism, Buddhism, Sikhism, and Hinduism. The idea behind reincarnation is that you will enter your new form to be a better person in this unique chance at life. You will try to do better than you did in the previous life. How you lived your last life will determine how you will come back to your new life. People who did not try to act as good, decent people in their previous lives might return as a bug or a weed. People who lived as good people will return to a more pleasant experience than the one they had before. The karma that a person collects during their incarnations will determine what form their new life will take. A person who has collected more negative karma than positive karma throughout their reincarnations will need to keep returning to active life until they achieve karmic balance. Someone with more negative karma has not learned to live a righteous life and let go of their ego.

A person will find salvation after death when they finally learn to live the most moral and ethical incarnation that they can live. The form of salvation that they are looking for is not to be born again, because this level of liberation is the real goal of reincarnation. Coming back endlessly in one form after another is not the way most people want to spend eternity. The ultimate goal of reincarnation is to stop being born again and moving into the astral plane.

# CHAPTER 5
## *Opening Your Third Eye Chakra*

The sixth of the seven internal chakras is known as the Third Eye Chakra, located between your physical eyes, directly in the center of your forehead. All of your in-depth knowledge and powers of intuition reside in this chakra. The ability to naturally have and use the sixth sense is born into every one, but most people will lose the ability to use it somewhere during childhood. Small children will see and know things that other people, especially adults, will not be able to see and understand. Little children believe that anything is possible because they have not yet learned the ways of the cynical nature of the world. They believe in everything, so then they will be receptive to everything brought to them by their Third Eye. Adults have mostly lost the ability to use the power that the Third Eye will get because they usually don't believe in what they can't see. Once you open your Third Eye and become more receptive to the forces that are lying dormant inside of you, then you will have the ability to be a fantastic receptor for messages from outside of this physical world.

Developing your Third Eye will bring you a level of spiritual awareness that might be overwhelming if there is not a solid foundation in the five internal chakras that are below the Third Eye. When you have done that, and you have opened the Third eye, then you will be more able to see yourself and the world around you, with the inner knowing we possess. Your Third Eye will affect many things in your life. It will influence whether or not you will meet your goals that are related to your deepest desires. It will help you to balance reason and emotion. It will help you to know whether you are moving forward in life or if you are stagnant. You will have a sense of the bigger picture that life presents to you. And it gives you the ability to form gut feelings that are accurate in their predictions.

All of the chakras have unique things that they will relate to, and these are known as correspondences. With the Third eye Chakra, its Sanskrit name is Ajna, which means 'to perceive.' The corresponding color of the Third Eye is indigo, and its corresponding symbol is a lotus flower with ninety-six petals. The aura layer of the Third Eye is the Celestial Body. It works well with all of the elements, but it mostly prefers light. Its goals are to understand and have a psychic perception, and also to use intuition and imagination. The Third Eye also works well with all of the senses, but it mainly prefers the sense of sight. Its corresponding zodiac signs are Sagittarius and Pisces, and its associated planets are Neptune, Mercury, and Venus. The owl and the butterfly are the animals that are associated with the Third Eye Chakra. It responds well to certain essential oils like patchouli, rosemary, vetiver, basil, and jasmine. It also works well with individual crystals and stones such as opal, sapphire, indigo, rainbow moonstone, and lapis lazuli. For foods that correspond to this chakra, look for colors in blue and purple like blueberries, blackberries, purple sweet potatoes, purple kale, grapes, purple cabbage, and eggplant.

Every chakra has its own emotional and physical areas that it directly corresponds to and directly influences. If your Third Eye Chakra is blocked, then you will most likely struggle to find faith in your purpose in life. You might feel as if you and your efforts are insignificant, or that there is no point in you being here or trying to contribute. You will probably struggle to make meaningful decisions. You may also work with trying to learn new ideas or concepts, and you might feel clumsy or have trouble sleeping. On the physical side, you will feel pain in your sinuses, back, and legs. Your eyes will often hurt or feel uncomfortable, and you may be prone to having headaches, especially migraines.

When your Third Eye is open and well-balanced, you will have the ability to connect to your intuitive wisdom and to see deeply into your soul and heart. You will be able to see how all things and all people are connected, and knowing this will help you navigate your way through life. You will be able to trust your innate intuition, and you will enjoy tremendous benefits from it. You will have a powerful and wealthy spiritual foundation that is supported by your understanding and awareness of the world. Awakening your Third Eye Chakra is the first step in being able to tap into all other forms of psychic awareness.

All things that need to pass to you from the outside world will need to go through your Third Eye. It is the bridge that lies between you and the outside world. When your Third Eye Chakra is opened, it will allow you to see what is real, even if those things are clouded by illusion and drama. If this chakra is feeling unhealthy, then you will find it challenging to learn new skills, use your intuition, recall important facts, or even trust your inner voice. When any of the lower chakras are imbalanced, it will make the Third Eye Chakra imbalanced as well, and this can make you feel more judgmental, introverted, and dismissive toward other people. But even if your Third Eye is not currently open, there are methods for reopening it that will soon enable you to be able to use this important chakra.

## Dietary Habits

Besides the purple and blue foods, other dietary habits will affect your third Eye Chakra. Cacao (not cocoa) is full of antioxidants that will improve the blood flow to this chakra. It also likes foods that are rich in Omega-3 fatty acids like avocado, salmon, and walnuts. All fruits, but especially blackberries and blueberries, contain antioxidants and flavonoids that will help to decrease your blood pressure, so that more and better circulation will be available to your Third Eye. Prunes and plums have phenols that fight off the free radicals that can attack the area that hold the Third Eye.

The purple vegetables like purple cabbage, purple onions, purple kale, and eggplant carry a variety of different polyphenols that help to reduce inflammation in your body. Inflammation will hinder the flow of blood and oxygen to the Third Eye. While flaxseed, fish, and nuts aren't purple, they do contain Omega-3 fatty acids that will help to lower the risk that you might develop depression and dementia, two conditions that will hamper the working of the Third Eye.

## Meditation

Meditation has many benefits for your body. It will help you concentrate better, channel your energies more efficiently, and clear the toxins out of your body. It can also help you and your Third Eye to be more self-aware and active so that your level of consciousness will shift into higher states with each session of meditation. This will help you to operate at your fullest capacity by removing worries and anxiety. Meditation is one of the best and easiest methods for activating your Third Eye. It will help to boost your clarity, improve your concentration, and focus on your mind.

Just like any other form of meditation, Third Eye meditation will require you to be present at the moment. You will need to surround yourself with soothing vibrations and sounds while keeping yourself in a calm environment. Begin your session by sitting in a position that you find comfortable, either on the floor or on a chair. While most pictures of people meditating show them sitting cross-legged on a pillow on the floor, you do not need to try to do this if you physically can't. Not everyone was meant to sit on the floor and get back up again! Sitting in a chair or on some other piece of furniture is a perfectly acceptable alternative. The important thing about where and how you are sitting is that you need to sit somewhere that you can sit upright. Your spine needs to be straight and tall. Keep your shoulders relaxed and lay your hands on your knees or softly in your lap. Open yourself to the positive energy by relaxing your face, stomach, and jaw.

Bring your thumb and your index finger together softly and then gently close your eyes. Meditation is a practice of grace and gentleness. Breathe slowly while inhaling and exhaling through your nose. While your eyes are close, try to look upward, in the direction of your Third Eye. Concentrate on this spot while you continue to breathe slowly. Continue breathing and concentrating on the location of your Third Eye until you can detect a light blue or white light that will begin to surround you. As this light starts to cover you, let yourself begin to succumb to its power. This will take you into the area of metaphysical healing, where your concentration will be at its most effective level because it will be at its highest level. While you are in this state, you will want to let go of any bad energies that you are holding. Let your emotions and thoughts go and just focus on maximizing the potential of your Third Eye chakra. Your priority right now is your focus.

Try to hold your meditation for at least ten minutes and preferably more if you can do so. Peaceful music and soft lighting can help you to stay in the reflection. Set some type of timer before you start so that you are not tempted to watch the clock, and you can concentrate on your meditation. End your session of meditation, just put your palms together gently and take a deep, cleansing breath and let it out slowly. Try to do this meditation daily, either first thing in the morning or just before you go to bed.

# Affirmations

An affirmation is a positive word or thought that you would say to yourself, silently or out loud, to combat the negative thoughts you might be having. When you recite affirmations every day, you will be able to keep your chakras balanced, especially the Third Eye chakra. You will become healthier every time you repeat your daily affirmations. The Third Eye chakra prefers assertions that correspond to seeing, both physical and emotional sight. Every chakra has certain theme words that trigger its opening, and for the Third Eye chakra, those theme words are 'I see,' 'I envision,' and 'I imagine." Use the theme words for the Third Eye chakra to create the affirmations that are uplifting and positive, to help you open your Third Eye chakra. Here are a few commitments that you can use to get started.

- I look for guidance and wisdom in all situations.
- The guidance that my third Eye gives me is excellent and safe.
- I embrace my new psychic abilities.
- The answers that I will need are inside of me, and I need to look for them.
- I will forgive and release the things of the past.
- I am the source of love for myself.
- I feel that everything is getting better in my world.
- I hear the voice of my soul speaking to me.
- I see my spiritual truth and ability.
- I will use my intuition for my own higher good.
- I know my higher self, and I will see my higher truth.
- My possibilities are unlimited.
- I will create my reality consciously and with insight.
- I will listen to my intuition when it speaks to me.
- My life is developing the way it was meant to.
- I can capture the larger picture of my life.
- I can see past all of the illusion and drama.
- My imagination is highly creative.
- There is a new vision available for my mind.
- I will expand my awareness.
- Every soul has its light, and I can see it.

- I can see the spiritual path I need to take.
- There are new challenges before me, and I can see them.
- I will only dwell in the present.

## Yoga

Yoga poses are beneficial for all parts of the body, including the forehead, where the Third Eye is located. Your Third Eye chakra is where you will find all of your intuition, which everyone has, although not everyone has the confidence to trust their intuition. When you learn to trust your intuition, you will need to go beyond the limits of what is logical and literal. You will need to start to trust your usual perception. When you have a feeling of intuition, you have the feeling of being drawn to those things that are good for you, even if your consciousness wants to resist it. When you open your Third Eye, you will be able to reconnect with who you are. You will then have the ability to navigate your physical world with compassion, kindness, and patience for yourself and others.

Practicing yoga will help to open your Third Eye chakra. To begin, you will first spend a few minutes, turning your gaze to look toward your Third Eye. Cosmic consciousness is provided through this gateway to the physical body. Yoga poses will help you to expand your inner knowing so that you will be able to recognize the symbols and signs that pop up along your path that will guide you toward your life's purpose.

Begin your yoga practice with a pose that is known as Downward Facing Dog. On your yoga mat, get down on the floor on your knees and hands. Make sure that you keep your knees directly under your hips, and your palms are on the floor or the mat slightly in front of your shoulders. Breathe out and lift your knees off the floor. When you first come up keep your knees bent just a little bit and your heels off of the floor. Press your tailbone upward toward the ceiling, breathing in while you do this. Then exhale and push your thighs back while your knees go straight, but not locked.

Make your arms straight, but do not lock your elbows. Keep your head between your upper arms, but keep your neck firm, do not let your head dangle. Stay in this pose for ten to thirty seconds before moving on to the next pose.

Now from Downward Facing Dog, you will move directly into a pose that is called Warrior I. While still in the Down Dog position, step your right foot forward and keep your left foot firmly on the floor. Take a deep breath in and stand up to come into the part that is known as Warrior I. Breath out while you place your fingers together behind your back. Breathe deeply in while you bend forward, putting your right shoulder against the inside of your right knee and pull your palms, with the fingers still together, gently up over your head. Let your shoulders, neck, and head stay firm but relaxed.

Let your arms drift back down as you stand up, and then move your right leg around to stand level with your left leg. Keep your legs spread widely apart. You will now move into the pose that is known as Humble Warrior. Keep your hands behind your back with your fingers placed together as before. Then bend to the front at the waist and lift your hands into the air, keeping the fingers together. Then let go of your fingers from behind your back and reach down and grab each of your big toes with your hands, left hand on left toe, and right hand on the right toe. Stay in this pose for ten to thirty seconds and then put your hands on your hips and slowly rise to a standing position. Bring your feet back together and then fold forward and put your hands on the floor, moving back into the Down Dog position.

While you are still in the Down Dog position, move your left foot forward so that it is in between your hands that are on the mat or floor. Do the Warrior sequence on the left side of your body. Then place your left foot back in line with the right foot, keeping your feet spread far apart. Reach to the front with your right hand and put it flat on the ground about two feet in front of your feet, moving into the Wide-Legged Forward Fold. Hold in this position for ten to thirty seconds, and then repeat this on the left side.

Keep practicing with your yoga positions and work to learn new ones. You can do yoga yourself by yourself at home by watching videos on the television. You can also find a class nearby if that is what you would prefer.

## Sound Frequency

There is a unique corresponding frequency for each of the seven internal chakras. Each of the chakras will vibrate at its frequency, and you can learn how to manipulate and influence the frequencies of the chakras so that you can open and balance them and keep them healthy. You are loaded with numerous different frequencies, since every cell in your body has the unique frequency that it will vibrate at. To heal your chakras by using sound frequency, you will need to find sounds on the same frequency as the chakra that you are trying to heal. Once you find the appropriate sound, you will just need to spend some time listening to it while you relax and let the sound frequency do its work. All sound levels are measured in Hz, which is the abbreviation for hertz unit. One hertz unit is equal to one unit of the frequency of the sound. One hertz unit is one vibration, or cycle, of the sound in a second.

Your Third Eye Chakra prefers a frequency of 852 Hz. Music and sound that is set to this frequency will help you replace your negative thoughts with positive thoughts. This frequency is ideal for awakening your intuition and inner strength, which are vital when you are opening your Third Eye. This frequency will also help to calm you when you are feeling anxious or nervous. Listening to this music will help you communicate with your higher self and live in harmony with the Universe.

## Essential Oils

Essential oils are often used to open and balance the Third Eye chakra. When the right essential oils are used, they will open this chakra to give you clear seeing, spiritual insight, and clarity of thought. On the spiritual level, the Third eye chakra controls your ability to see connections with others and the more profound truth, understand and trust your intuition, and see straight through illusion and drama. On a mental level, this chakra will help you make better decisions, understand symbolic language, think abstractly, and have good memory skills. On the emotional level, your Third Eye will help rid you of nightmares, make you feel powerful in any situation, and keep you free from delusional thinking. On the physical level, you will enjoy a healthier brain, eyes, and pituitary and pineal gland.

Essential oils will embody the healing properties and frequencies of the plants they came from. These properties and frequencies will work on all types of living beings.

Lavender works to calm your strong emotions and release the pent up energy that your body is holding in. This essential oil will allow for all of the forces of life to flow freely through your body. This oil will allow peace and calm to arise during sleep or meditation, helping you to connect with the astral spirits and the Divine.

Geranium is one of the most valuable essential oils for circulatory issues. It will stimulate the circulation in your brain, and it will also enhance the flow of blood to your pituitary and pineal glands. Geranium can relax and calm your nervous system, and it will help strengthen the vital energy in your body. It is also good to use for those people who spend too much time relying on the left side of their brain. The essential oil of geranium works to bridge the gap between the right mind and the left brain hemispheres to bring to you precise abilities to see well and a more balanced perspective.

Orange Blossom made into an essential oil, which is also known as neroli, is both a tonic and a sedative, and it will work to regulate the function of your nervous system. Neroli has a delicate and sweet citrusy, floral scent. It is often utilized as a natural remedy for shock, depression, and anxiety. Neroli will help to bring more equilibrium to both your mind and your heart, as it is sufficient for both of these centers of energy.

Clary Sage has been used for centuries to treat diseases of the eye. As an essential oil it will help to calm your mind and is especially suitable for treating headaches, especially migraines. Clary Sage essential oil is also used for treating seizures and in the management of epilepsy and autism.

Rose essential oil has a relaxing and calming effect, and it also has the highest vibrational frequency of all of the essential oils. Its high level of vibration makes it ideal for helping to align your physical body with your subtle body to create harmony and balance. This oil will also create an inner sense of well-being while it elevates and stimulates your mind.

Chamomile essential oil will allow you to see the impulses and drives of your ego while it works to soothe and calm your nervous system. It will help you to understand that your projections and purposes, and the various patterns of your ego, are not who you are inside. It will help you see your ego from another perspective and begin to remove yourself from it. This is one of the skills that are vital for you to be able to open your Third Eye.

Melissa essential oil will allow you to access higher vibrations and higher realms while you get in touch with extraordinary realities. It helps to stimulate your pineal gland.

Carrot Seed made into an essential oil is one of the most important of the essential oils that are used on the Third Eye. It has been utilized for centuries to treat diseases of the physical eye. This oil is one essential oil that will allow you to see the reality of the here and now, while it helps you to remain grounded in that reality. It helps to harmonize your physical body with your subtle body. With this harmony, you will be able to experience spiritual insights and visions while staying present in this plane of material existence.

Palo Santo, made into an essential oil, is also known as Holy Wood, and it is used in ceremonies for purification. This essential oil is burned for cleansing auras and as incense. You will use Palo Santo essential oil while you are praying, meditating, or conducting a cleansing ritual. It will enhance your ability to perceive other realms, and it will also heighten your connection to the Divine and your spiritual awareness. It has a rich and sweet aroma

Jasmine essential oil is known in India as the Queen of the Night. It is often used in rituals for healing and magic, and it is associated with the moon. Since the aroma of this essential oil is incredibly uplifting, it will allow you to gain access to the deepest layers of your soul and to deal with the emotional pain that you have repressed there. Jasmine enhances your connection to the Universe and your powers of intuition. While it is compelling for stimulating your senses, it has a sweetly floral aroma.

Bay Laurel that is made into an essential oil is one of the classic essential oils, and it is used to open your doors of perception and heighten your awareness. When you use Bay Laurel essential oil, your powers of clairaudience, clairvoyance, and clairsentience will all be amplified and enhanced. The ancient Greeks liked to use Bay Laurel to increase a seer's ability for prophecy and divination. Bay Laurel essential oil will give you an awakened awareness and a more holistic perception by helping to connect your creative right brain and your rational left brain.

If you are using essential oil to open your Third Eye, one of the best ways to do this is to apply a few drops of the oil to the area where the chakra is so that you would put a few drops in the middle of your forehead. Essential oil is too concentrated, and therefore too strong, to be put directly on your skin. It will need to be added to a carrier oil like baby oil before you place it on your skin. There are varied and exciting ways in which you can use essential oils in your daily life.

- In a small spray bottle of water, put a few drops of the essential oil and use it to spray around your room.
- Use a diffuser to add a few drops to and let the scent fill the room.
- Place five to seven drops of your favorite essential oil on a tissue or a ball of cotton and place it in a bowl next to you.
- Drop a few drops of essential oil into a cup of boiling water for the aroma.
- Mix ten to twelve drops of your chosen essential oil into vegetable oil and then add this to a hot bath.
- Blend six to twelve drops of essential oil into an unscented face or body lotion.
- Place a few drops of essential oil on a tissue and slip it inside of your pillowcase just before going to bed.

## Crystals

Using the healing power of crystals is another way that you can use to open your Third Eye. It is effortless to use crystals in your daily life.

- Lie flat on your back and set the crystal of your choice in the middle of your forehead while you meditate or say or think affirmations.
- Hold the crystal in your hand and stare at it while you meditate or say affirmations.

- Set the crystals on the side of the bathtub while you bathe, or drop them into the water.
- Decorate your home or office with various Third Eye friendly crystals.
- Wear jewelry made of the crystals of your choice.
- Carry a crystal or two in your purse or pocket.

Several different crystals will be your best choices for opening your Third Eye.

Amethyst crystal is also called the stone of spirituality. It is a beautiful purple stone that will awaken your mind while it is calming your soul. This crystal will help to open your psychic abilities and help to lift you to the next level of spiritual development by reminding you that you are one with the Divine. The powerful spiritual energies that this stone emits make it the most popular and most common stone for soothing and opening the Third Eye. Amethyst will help to bring balance and harmony when your Third Eye is out of balance. It will aid in strengthening your psychic abilities by bringing clarity to your mind. You can also use a piece of amethyst if you need to heal disorders of your nervous system or your brain, as well as problems with addiction. Amethyst will also calm your stress and frustration as it works to calm your mind. It will allow you to have a more mindful session of meditation. It will also help you recall your dreams and encourage astral travel. Amethyst will give you the patience and wisdom to understand your abilities, and it will help you avoid having nightmares and other negative dreams.

Clear Quartz is often called the master healer of stones because it can be used as a substitute for any rock or crystal of any color. This stone is the only one that you can use on all seven of your internal chakras. The primary purpose of clear quartz is to charge other crystals with its vibrational energies. It will help you awaken your inner abilities by doubling the strengths of all stones you use with it. Your powers of thought and your intentions that you put out to the Universe will be much stronger when you use a clear quartz crystal. The Universe will be able to hear you clearly so that it can assist you. It will also act as your teacher and guide while you are on your spiritual journey, helping you to stay straight on the path to enlightenment. Clear quartz is also a powerful form of psychic protection. When you carry a piece of clear quartz with you or wear it as jewelry, you will be protecting yourself from the negative energies that other people put off. The clear quartz crystal will also help you reduce your negative emotions like ill thoughts, envy, and jealousy.

Labradorite is a very highly protective and spiritual stone that will enhance your psychic abilities when your Third Eye is awakened. It will also shield you from any negative energies and influences and protect your aura from intrusion. This stone is a favorite for psychics and empaths, and since most psychics are empaths, this might be the perfect crystal for you to use. Sometimes referred to as the stone of transformation, labradorite is a highly supportive stone. It will work with your Third Eye to give you a clearer understanding of the intuitive purposes of the struggles and challenges that you might face in life. When you are meditating, labradorite will bring balance into your intuition and intellect. It will also work with your vibrational energies to improve your abilities to discern the truth in all matters. It will also help to regulate your metabolism as well as helping to relieve illnesses of your brain and your eyes.

Lapis lazuli stone has been used and revered since ancient times. This dark blue stone is thought to be the stone of enlightenment and illumination, which makes it a perfect crystal to use with your Third Eye chakra. The flecks of gold in the dark blue stone remind many people of the idea that the night sky is infinite and possible for everything. This stone will help you along the way during your psychic journey. The blue color of the stone will help you detach your consciousness from this realm, and it will help you to open your mind. And this stone is a courageous protector, which it does by using its vibrational energy to connect your mind to the pathways of the soul stars. This will give your mind a form of mental transit along the way, which will help to bind you to the stars and the heavens. And lapis lazuli will work to condition your energy to a higher level of vibrations so that you will be able to improve your progress in spiritual matters. It will work to connect you with the spirit guides and enhance your ability to recall your dreams.

Moldavite is one stone that will work with all seven of your internal chakras, but it works best with the Third Eye chakra. It is quite useful for enhancing your metaphysical abilities. Moldavite will suffice to clear the blockages that are keeping your Third Eye closed, to give it the correct function. This functionality will include spiritual awakening, increased synchronicity, more vivid dreams, and a deeper meaning in your life. Moldavite will also encourage you to be open to new perceptions in your life. It will enhance the flow of energy to your body and mind and help to bridge the gap between the two. Moldavite does work quickly and intensely, so it will need to be used with caution.

Sodalite is a calming stone that will silence the chaotic and negative thoughts that keep you distracted so that your mind will remain calm. While the blue hues, if the stone works to calm your mind, the white veining in the stone will help to align your mind to your higher self, allowing you to begin your psychic journey quickly. This crystal is highly spiritual, and it will work to clear away hallucinations and other mental debris that block the information pathways in your mind. It will enhance your intuitive and spiritual perception. Sodalite also works to rebuild your self-esteem and self-trust and helps you to have a healthy emotional balance in your life by removing your fear and guilt. Sodalite also rejects negativity and seeks the truth in all matters, which will allow you to defend the things that you believe in and always be true to yourself. It will help you to balance your thoughts and feelings.

Moonstone helps you to reconnect to the psychic abilities that you have shut down because of fear and misunderstanding. Moonstone holds the ultimate power of the moon, so it is even more potent at night. It will also keep you well protected at night, especially when you are traveling. The stone will help you to regulate your internal body clock and also work to absorb the negativities and tensions that you collect from your surroundings. Since much of the energy in moonstone is feminine, it is particularly recommended for women to use.

Iolite gives off an energy that heightens your sixth sense and increases your inner vision. It will work on your Third Eye to activate it as well as balance and heal it. Iolite is gentle but powerful enough to help you recognize destructive patterns in your life. This crystal will let you release any of your controlling or domineering tendencies. If you relax with iolite sitting directly on your Third Eye, it will enhance your self-confidence and self-trust while opening up your psychic abilities. It will also assist you in possessing greater mental clarity.

## Other Methods for Opening Your Third Eye

There are also other methods for opening your Third Eye. Some of them are listed here:
- Explore new ideas and beliefs that are outside your comfort zone. When your Third Eye is closed, it prefers to be oblivious to the world around it.

- Stop your consumption of processed foods and junk foods. Your body was not made to digest the amounts of sugar, carbs, and fat that are in the typical Western diet.
- Spend some quiet time meditating with a cup of tea made from one of the herbs that support the health of your Third Eye. Some of these include passionflower, rosemary, Ginkgo Biloba, and Gotu Kola.
- Practice mindfulness. Overthinking is one of the symptoms of a Third Eye that is not functioning correctly. Try to keep your thoughts grounded in the present and in the place where you are.
- Take some time to explore your own core beliefs. Sometimes our thoughts and opinions are the cause of a closed or unhealthy Third eye. Make sure that your views are not keeping you locked in a restrictive mindset that is preventing your Third Eye from opening.
- Write your feelings down in a journal. The Third Eye is much attuned to emotions, especially positive ones. Writing them down will help you to become more comfortable with your thoughts and beliefs.

Anyone can open their Third Eye if they genuinely want to. It will take dedication, and you will need to have the willingness to dig into your soul and bring up things you might prefer never to see again. This dedication will help you make the changes that are needed in your life so that you can open and utilize the power of your Third Eye. You will find that the effort is worth it, and you will receive an abundance of mental clarity that will serve you for the remainder of your life.

# CHAPTER 6
*The Pineal Gland And The Third Eye*

In your brain, there is a small endocrine gland that is known as the pineal gland. This gland is the gland that is responsible for the production of the hormone melatonin, which is the hormone that is responsible for putting you to sleep when it is time to go to sleep. This gland is shaped like a little pine cone, which is where it got its name. You will find this gland very near the center of your brain, in between the left hemisphere and the right hemisphere. The melatonin that is created by the pineal gland had many essential functions for the central nervous system. It's most important function is to regulate patterns of sleep, since the production of melatonin is inhibited by light and stimulated by darkness.

While the total role of the pineal gland is still not understood, the ancient traditions and cultures of the world already had an understanding of this gland and its importance. In Taoism, the pineal gland was considered to be the eye of heaven and the eye of the mind. The pineal gland was the seat of clairvoyance and intuition for the ancient Hindus. And the Buddhists referred to the pineal gland as the symbol of spiritual awakening. There were numerous references to the pineal region and the Third Eye in the writings of the ancient Egyptians. The ancient Greeks felt that the pineal gland was the direct connection to thought. They thought the pineal gland was the connecting link between the psychic dimension and the physical world. They referred to the pineal gland as the Third Eye for a straightforward reason. In early versions of autopsies, when the pineal gland was dissected, it was found to be filled with structures that looked precisely like the cones and rods in the retina of the human eye. They understood that light, like sunlight, would flow through the skulls of smaller creatures like fish and birds, and this light would stimulate the pineal gland. The opinion was that the same effect happened in the brains of humans, so the pineal gland became known as the Seeing Eye inside of the mind. They believed that humans would receive messages along with the light directly into the pineal gland.

The pineal gland was once believed to be directly related to the Third Eye Chakra, and it was a useful tool that was revered by the ancient seers and mystics. Much of this power has been lost in the past few centuries as people have stopped tapping into the energy that flows between the pineal gland and the Third Eye. Most people will know that they are not living up to their fullest potential. Even knowing this, most of this knowledge is in the subconscious. This means that you might realize that you are not living up to your full potential, but you don't connect your shortcomings to the reality of the situation. But you do know the difference between the two facts. There are reasons why humans don't operate at the top of their inner power. The human mind doesn't always function the way it is supposed to. Like many other glands, the pineal gland does not work the way it was intended to. You possess the power to change that if you simply follow a few essential steps.

## Decalcify and Detox the Pineal Gland

Unlike the rest of your brain, the pineal gland is not isolated by the blood and brain barrier from the rest of the body. The pineal gland gets a large amount of blood flow, with its blood flow being second only to your kidneys. Over time the pineal gland begins to collect calcium deposits from the environment, the foods you eat, and the things that you drink. This causes your pineal gland to slow down in its function of creating melatonin. Then it will stop following your circadian rhythms, and you will find it difficult to sleep at night and stay awake in the daytime.

Poor sleep habits will reduce your mental performance and damage your cognitive function. You can also be more prone to developing diseases. Since the pineal gland is the connection for your body to the natural world, disconnecting it will cause people to be disconnected from each other, the rest of the world, and their instincts. If your pineal gland is not functioning completely, you will make poor decisions and fall prey to false messages and belief systems. When your pineal gland is calcified, you will lose most or all of your tremendous potential. You will need to decalcify your pineal gland to begin the process of your reawakening.

You will need to do three things to decalcify your pineal gland. You will first need to eliminate the environmental causes and the foods that cause calcification in your pineal gland. Then you will need to remove the calcification that is already built up. There are many different ways to do this, and most of them involve using certain supplements to boost your body systems. Then you will need to keep yourself in an environment that will keep your pineal gland healthy and functioning.

# Restore your Circadian Rhythm

Some people like to think that the less time they spend sleeping will leave them more time for being productive, but the exact opposite is true. Those people who know the value of a night of good sleep and regularly get the amount of sleep that they need will be much more productive than those people who struggle to stay awake. You can increase your physical energy, expand your cognitive capacities, enhance the power of your memory, and upgrade your mental performance. Still, without the proper amount of sleep each night, none of these methods will work for you.

Your circadian rhythm is the twenty-four-hour cycle of all of the biological activities that are linked to the natural periods of darkness and light. Another term for circadian rhythm is your biological clock. Your physical light meter is your pineal gland. It creates and secretes the hormone melatonin, the hormone that is responsible for the regulation of your circadian rhythm. The exposure of light to your open eyes is the trigger that tells your body how much melatonin to make. Your pineal gland will increase its production of melatonin during the darkness of night, and it will decrease its production during the daylight hours. Melatonin does more in your body than just regulate your circadian rhythm. It also promotes proper healing of damaged tissues, supports the immune response of your cells, works as an anti-inflammatory agent in your body, helps to reduce chronic levels of pain in your body, and it helps you sleep.

Before the use of artificial light, people went outside during the day and stayed inside when it was dark, and the pineal gland knew how to function correctly. The sun was the primary source of light for most people. When people worked under the natural time clock that the sun and the moon provided, their bodies were able to stay in alignment with their circadian rhythms. Now that the world is ruled by artificial light, the pineal gland has lost most of its natural ability to function. And your sleep will suffer because of it.

So while you will probably not be able to ditch all of the artificial light in your own life, there are things you can do to minimize its use and help you get back to a more natural world of light. Lower the brightness on all of your computer screens as far as you possibly can. During the day, go outside every few hours and look up at the sky, don't look directly at the sun. Take a break from staring at electronics whenever you can. And when it is time to go to sleep, make the room as dark as you possibly can. Even a small bit of light will confuse your pineal gland into thinking it is time to stop producing melatonin, and this will disrupt your ability to fall asleep and stay asleep.

## Activate the Pineal Gland

Once you have decalcified and detoxed your pineal gland, and restored your circadian rhythms, then you will need to reactivate your pineal gland so that it will be fully ready to work when you have opened your Third Eye. You are responsible for your journey to higher development and awakening. Follow these steps to activate your pineal gland fully.

The most traditional way to reactivate your pineal gland is by using meditation. Your pineal gland is quite sensitive to the bioelectrical energy signals of dark and light in the environment. You can use meditation to activate this form of energy and direct it to the pineal gland so that you can stimulate it and help it to open fully. A proper meditation for your pineal gland is effortless. Sit somewhere that you are comfortable and relaxed and close your eyes. Focus steadily on your breath and notice how your breath slows just because you are paying attention to it. Once your breathing has slowed, then focus your attention on the area where your Third Eye belongs. Do not try to force your breath and your mind to relax because that will only make you more energetic. Just sit calmly and relax as much as possible. If you expect or want a specific result, you will only succeed in blocking the very energy you wish to entice.

This meditation works because you are focusing your internal energy on your pineal gland and not waiting for something from an outside source. The relaxed focus you adopt will let you sink deeper into relaxation and the stimulation of the pineal gland. Meditating is another way to cause the pineal gland to secrete melatonin. When you begin to feel slight pressure or a pulsing sensation in the area between your Third Eye and your pineal gland, then you will know the meditation is working.

While you have probably been told all of your life that staring directly at the sun is dangerous, when you do it for short periods, it is beneficial. If you are genuinely committed to the idea of tapping into your higher potential, then you will need to be ready to question everything that you think you now know. You will find that most of the things that you have learned are somewhat limited in their scope, or are false. Staring at the sun directly, or sun gazing, is one of these things. It is an ancient technique that will offer you powerful benefits. The theory behind the practice is that you will absorb the energy of the sun directly through your skin and eyes.

The safest time for you to practice sun gazing is early in the morning, as the sun is beginning to rise because the sun will be closer to earth at that time and will not be as strong. Stand barefoot so that you are in touch with the ground, and do not look through a window; you need to be outside to do this. Begin with looking at the sun for just ten seconds at a time and slowly build your tolerance for up to thirty minutes. You can partially close your eyes if you feel the sun is too bright. If the day is cloudy, then stare at the spot in the clouds that is in front of the sun. The theory behind this technique is that the sun is the force of life for all things, and by staring directly at the sun; you will collect large amounts of energy for your pineal gland and Third Eye.

Sungazing might also help you with another method for activating your pineal gland, and that method is fasting. People who regularly sun gaze report that they feel less hunger, and they find that fasting is easier for them. Periodic fasting is right for your body in so many ways. It will increase your levels of human growth hormone, which helps your body regenerate, and it will help lower your risk of developing many chronic diseases. There are many different schedules that you can follow if you would like to give intermittent fasting a try. Fasting will also help to detoxify your body, which will help to reactivate your pineal gland.

Practicing the ancient art of Qigong (chee-gong) is another method for reactivating your pineal gland. The exercises serve to increase the flow of energy through your body and your sensitivity to that energy. You will learn how to move the energy around in your body by using breathing and gentle motions. Then you can move this energy with intent by using just the power of your mind. Most people have blocked energy channels that prevent the energy of life to flow freely through their bodies. These blockages prevent the fuel from reaching the parts of your body where it is most needed. When the energy can flow freely, it can get all aspects of the body, including the pineal gland.

When you think about activating your pineal gland, you are talking about bringing all of the power in your mind to actualization. This power will allow you to use all of the parts of your mind together. Once you have reactivated your pineal gland and you can open your Third Eye, a whole new world will open up for you. You will begin to perceive your reality quite differently. You will start to notice more of your unconscious behavior. This process will alert you to many new facts about your own life and the Universe around you. You will learn many truths about life itself that you were not able to know before. This path is a new adventure for you, and the door is always open.

# CHAPTER 7
## *Reiki Healing And The Third Eye*

Reiki healing uses energy to heal the physical body and the subtle body. Reiki healers use the palms of their hands to lie on the patient in a technique known as palm healing. The word Reiki is derived from two words that mean divine vitality. The theory behind reiki is that the practitioner can bring down the dynamism of the divine by using themselves as the medium and their hands as the instrument. It is a subtle method of guiding your life force using the energy from the divine and the Universe.

All the energy that flows through all living beings is the force of Reiki. Healers will practice with the intention that all people hold within them the ability to heal themselves if they can connect with the appropriate healing energy. This energy is in you, and you can use it to heal yourself and other people. It would help if you had your power to be healthy and flowing freely through your body. When your energy flows freely, then your mind and body will vibrate positively with good health and strength. When your life is blocked or stagnant, then you will experience physical or emotional imbalances.

Reiki as a healing practice has been used since the late nineteenth century. Japanese monks used the techniques and taught them in their monasteries. Several different forms of Asian healing techniques provided the specific methods and techniques of Reiki. The basic concept is that imbalances of energy cause disease, and the body will heal itself when these imbalances are corrected. The idea is finding favor in the West and is widely used in Eastern medicine even today.

Modern practitioners use the same techniques that were taught centuries ago by the monks. The ancient concept of an infinite supply of energy for healing the body still rings true with Reiki healers. Those who have mastered the Reiki technique will use attunements, which is a process to teach others how to master Reiki themselves. During a session, the patient will lie down on a table, and the master will let their hands hover over the patient. Energy will flow through the master and down into the patient. Illness or injury will show in the patient where the power is blocked. The master will lay their hands over the blockage to allow the healing energy to release the jam.

Reiki will improve symptoms and conditions like insomnia, tension, headaches, and nausea. It will help to relieve your anxiety and depression, so it works to improve your mood. It can improve your self-confidence and self-esteem. You will be able to relax with better sleep patterns, and this will provide you with calm nerves and inner peace. Relieving your physical symptoms will help your emotional symptoms to improve. People with severe or chronic illnesses will enjoy relief from pain, anxiety, and fatigue.

Some masters will use crystals to make the Reiki session more powerful. They will place these crystals around your body, or on different points of your body, to let the energy from the crystals enhance the energy from the Reiki session. Some of the crystals more commonly used are rose quartz, amethyst, moonstone, topaz, tourmaline, and aquamarine.

Reiki is effective when used to heal the Third Eye chakra. Your entire body will benefit from the energy that is released when the Third Eye is healed. Your Third Eye has an important role in balancing your inner vision and emotional peace. The practitioner will use the Reiki techniques to release the blockage that is hampering the function of your Third Eye. Reiki also helps your mind be receptive to the energy of the divine that will flow to you through the Third Eye. Your mental state will greatly improve during the session, because your body will relax and your mind will cease activity. This will give you inner peace, and that will help you gain the perfect state that will allow the spirits to come to you. Once your Third Eye is opened then the energy of the Universe will flow through it to reside in you.

# CHAPTER 8
## *Psychic Abilities And Your Third Eye*

Now that your Third Eye is awakened to the possibilities of life, you will be able to take advantage of all of the new psychic abilities that will be available to you. People with psychic powers are nothing more than regular individuals who possess the abilities that go beyond the boundaries of the material world. These people can sense, feel, taste, hear, and see, and they have the power of intuition. Psychic skills are the ability to process the data that you receive from intangible and tangible stimuli on a profoundly physical, spiritual, or emotional level. Psychic abilities vary significantly in application and intensity.

Most psychic abilities are developed originally in childhood. Children see more, feel more, hear more, and notice more. Children are naturally more psychic because they believe everything is real, even spirits. When children grow older and are steered more in the direction of math and science and less in the way of imagination and creativity, they will lose their psychic abilities. Adults accept that the physical world is the only realm that exists. But your psychic skills are never lost, and you can quickly revive them with a little practice.

## Mahamudra Meditation

This meditation style is a form of highly intentional meditation that will help you realize your full potential after you have opened your Third Eye. The true nature of your abilities will not come from accidents, good luck, or willpower. Psychic skills need to be worked on, and this is where you can use Mahamudra meditation to hone your abilities. You can use this knowledge to do your practice for psychic openness. You will need to begin with understanding what this form of meditation is. There are three distinct parts to Mahamudra meditation. It starts with Ground Mahamudra, which will show you how to find the fundamental reality in your world and your mind. Path Mahamudra will teach you how to start on your practice of this form of meditation. Fruition Mahamudra shows where the path of this meditation will take you. When you have learned to work through all three parts, then you will experience the total picture of your journey of awakening that is known as Mahamudra.

Your mind is spacious, open, and transparent, and you will see this with a clear and steady focus after learning this meditation. In the beginning, you will not be able to see and enjoy your thoughts and emotions, as they will vaporize when you focus on them. There is wisdom in emptiness, and you will need to learn to recognize and accept this emptiness to realize your true potential. Your mind will be awakened and will become aware of the wisdom that the void allows inside. You must be able to empty your mind so that you can accept the knowledge of the divine after your Third Eye is open. This wisdom is what will bring you true enlightenment. Opening your Third Eye is just the first step. It is like opening the door to a house. Once the door is open, then people and things can come in, but the door must first be opened. This reality is what opening the Third Eye will do for you. It is just a means to an end, one step on the path to true enlightenment.

You will need to become familiar with how your mind will work now so that you can learn how to use it correctly, and this is what Mahamudra meditation will teach you. Your first glance into your mind will reveal a space where thoughts are poorly organized, and they are allowed to wander in all directions. Your mind will need guidance so that it will work correctly. Your first learning will be methods for bringing order and clarity to your mind and your thoughts. When you are mindful of the workings of your thought processes, then your awareness will become more precise and sharper. As your mind learns how to relax and expand, then you will inhabit a dimension open in the present. Mahamudra meditation will show you how to rest within the nature and openness of your mind and how to see clearly for the first time. With most reflections, you need to concentrate on an object or a thought, focusing your attention on one thing. Mahamudra meditation allows your mind to relax and clear itself in a natural state. The best description of this form of meditation is learning to release stress and relax while being mindful of the present. Although this kind of meditation might feel unnatural and stressful in the beginning, as you practice, you will become more comfortable with the techniques.

Find a place that is free of distractions and sit down and relax. Focus on how good it feels to sit there and relax. Feel your thoughts and your breath. Take as long as you need to sit quietly and relax, breathing slowly and deeply. Look directly in front of you with focus, letting your eyes see what is there and your mind understand what is there. Then gradually allow your vision to become unfocused so that you are looking more at the whole area in front of you but focused on nothing in particular. Quietly relax in this position for a few minutes. Accept without judgment or comment any emotions, thoughts, or feelings that come into your mind. It is normal for your mind to try to fill itself. The opinions and feelings are neither bad nor good; they are. Let your mind relax and accept what comes.

The object of this form of meditation is to focus on the clarity, emptiness, and awareness of your mind as it learns to relax and be receptive. You will understand the true nature of your mind while you are unfocused and open. Reflect on the space in your mind and the openness that lies within, while you are allowing your mind to be empty. You will gain clarity from the radiance that fills your mind. Sit calmly and star into space while your mind rests and becomes calm. Think of the new clarity in your mind. See and feel the emotions and thoughts that are nothing more than the natural expressions of an open mind. Acknowledge your thoughts, but do not let yourself feel them. A happy idea will not bring happiness, and an angry view will not bring anger. You are more concerned with not judging your thoughts than you are about having the thoughts. This acceptance will bring you awareness of the mind. Relax in the clarity of your mind while you stare into the space in front of you. Gradually let your eyes begin to refocus, and your mind comes back into the present. Sit quietly for a few more minutes before you go about your daily activities.

## Writing Automatically

When you are in an altered mental state such as a trance, you may be able to indulge in automatic writing. The ability to do this comes from a place that is outside of your conscious awareness, most often from another astral plane. Automatic writing might be the inner workings of your mind, or it might be the messages that you receive from spirits and angels through your Third Eye. It might also be the work of your subconscious relating to your subtle body or your higher self.

Working to perfect your automatic writing abilities will help you reap numerous benefits. You will develop a deeper trust in your instincts and intuition. You will feel supported and deeply understood. You will make contact with the spirit guides assigned to you so that you can know their perspectives and opinions. Your decisions will be smarter, and your intuition will be sharpened and better developed. And since you will have the ability to receive direction from higher powers, your daily life will be filled with clarity and precision.

Automatic writing will calm you while it works to open your mind. It is simple to execute and can be done anytime. Have your paper and pen ready when you sit down to relax, so you are prepared to write your responses. Think of a question that needs answering or a problem that you are experiencing. Write your question on the top of the paper. Now sit back and relax, opening your mind while you think of the item that you wrote down. Remain utterly relaxed in mind and body while you wait for answers. As the feelings and thoughts begin to come to you, let your writing flow freely onto the paper. Do not worry about grammar or syntax, but let the ideas flow from your mind, through your arm and hand, and down onto the paper. Do not proofread your work or add punctuation. Your writing may not make sense to anyone but you, but that is not what is essential. The critical part of this exercise is for you to become comfortable with receiving messages from the spirit world, and then letting those messages become thoughts that you can freely express through your writing. This is not a skill that you will immediately excel with. Automatic writing takes time and patience to develop, so do not be discouraged if your first few attempts do not give you the results you were hoping to have. Just keep following the steps, and soon you will be an expert at automatic writing.

When you form your question, make sure it is something that you need help with and not just a random thought. This technique might be the outlet you need, especially if you are struggling to receive messages through your newly opened Third Eye. Meditate before you begin your session if you need to so that your mind will be open and receptive. Make your question vital to you, since you will receive a better response if there is thought and emotion involved in the question. Choose the specific entity from which you want a reply. You can query your subtle body, your subconscious mind, a spirit guide, or the divine. It will be easier for them to form an answer if your question is simple. You will need to keep your session to just one problem, performing more sessions if you have more than one problem.

Let your mind relax fully before you begin. This relaxation is where the meditation will help you the most. You might find that this is the most challenging step since life today is so crazy sometimes. But it is vital that your mind is relaxed and clear when you begin. If your mind is cloudy or cluttered, you might not receive the exact messages you need. Any method will work to clear your mind if meditation does not work for you. Try using crystals or essential oils, or do a few yoga poses. Mindfulness and deep breathing might also help you.

Enter a light trance as you begin your session. A trance is a form of altered consciousness that is relatively easy to attain. It will allow your mind to relax fully. Your automatic writing will flow more quickly if your mind is relaxed. If you find it challenging to enter a trance, you can try some guided meditation or self-hypnosis. You can also enter a trance by listening to soft music, repeating a chant or mantra, or doing repetitive tasks.

Once you have entered your trance and the information is coming to you, do not try to stop it. As soon as you are ready, you can begin writing. It is okay if the words you write make no sense. Writing nonsense words is a good sign because it means that you have tapped into a flow of information that is outside of your conscious mind. If your conscious mind tries to intrude, ease it back into the trance. You might need to spend a few minutes getting back into your trance, and this is normal in the beginning. Just remain relaxed, and it will come back to you quickly. You might also need to adjust to the practice of writing, mostly if you usually text or type everything. Take the time to practice your automatic writing, and you will naturally improve.

Wait until the information stops flowing to you before you try to read what you have written. It will be easy for you to know when your session is over. The thoughts and feelings will stop coming to you, or your writing will just stop. When that happens, you can take the time to analyze what you have written. First, look for any phrases or words that make sense. Pick out any word that you have used more than once. You will not receive your information from simply reading what you have written, because it will not be written clearly in sentences and paragraphs. You will need to put all of the clues together to make sense of what you have written. And if the information you recorded on the paper makes absolutely no sense to you, then that might be the sign that you need to ask a different question or ask your question differently.

If the thoughts you recorded are disjointed and vague, that is a good sign that the ideas are coming from your divine source. When you write frantically, and the words make sense, that is a good sign that you are writing down the emotions in your mind and soul. Automatic writing will flow lightly across the paper, and the words will be nonsensical and a bit garbled. Keep practicing, and you will be able to make automatic writing work for you.

## Yoga for your Mind

Once your Third Eye is open, you will begin to receive messages from various sources. Sometimes your messages may come across as harsh or negative thoughts and emotions. When this happens, you probably need to spend some time stretching your mind so that it can continue to learn and grow. When your feelings cross over into your spiritual thoughts, you may need to take advantage of some mental yoga to help clear your mind. Mental yoga does for the mind what physical yoga does for the body. It will help you to stretch your mind and your emotions, clearing out excess toxins and unnecessary feelings and thoughts. Mental yoga might cause you some discomfort, but it will help bring you where you want to be.

Sometimes people think that, because their Third Eye is open and functioning, that their psychic abilities will naturally develop and display themselves on command. This rapid ability rarely happens. There will be some discomfort when you begin this journey, and that is needed for you to grow emotionally and spiritually. Mental yoga is made of three different ideas. You will first need to accept that your emotions are normal and acceptable. They are a natural part of you being human. Life will give you anger, happiness, sadness, and regret over your lifetime, and these are all-natural. You need to accept your emotions so that you can function better mentally and emotionally. Do not try to control your feelings or eliminate them; accept them. Examine your feelings without reacting to them or judging them, and use your natural curiosity to learn from your emotions, especially the negative ones. It is easy to understand why you are happy, but you also need to know why you have negative feelings. Your curiosity will engage your logic, and this will allow you to learn from your reactions to your emotions. Then you can harness that knowledge to create intelligent steps to move closer to your goals. You will find it easier to commit to actions and behaviors that will help you achieve your goals if you are not stressed about your reactions or trying to resist them.

Those people who study the ancient art of yoga as it was meant to be used know that yoga is not just about the poses. The traditional practice of yoga is not just a form of exercise that involves stretching and bending. The real benefit of yoga is the mental, psychological, and spiritual clarity it will give you. Yoga is a way of life with benefits for all areas of your life. The actual practice of yoga will keep you in a healthy frame of mind as it balances your mind as well as your body. Ashtanga yoga is one of the best yoga practices for keeping a clear mind and body. The principles of this discipline will guide you through an enlightened life. Ashtanga yoga is one of the oldest yoga disciplines and one of the most authoritative. Ashtanga yoga has eight different philosophies, called the eight limbs that will guide all aspects of your life. The philosophies deal with cultivating internal awareness, yoga poses, concentration, self-discipline, meditation, integrity, transcending the self, and controlling your breathing. Transcending the self is the eighth limb, and you will need to attain the other seven levels if you want to achieve the eighth one. Practicing Ashtanga yoga will bring you to the level of awareness that you want to accomplish with your newly opened Third eye.

With the first limb, you will focus on your behavior and how you conduct yourself as you travel through life. You will examine your integrity and your ethical standards, as you try to live your life in a manner that will allow you to be kind to others, treating others as you want to be treated. The second limb will teach you to remain spiritual while you learn self-discipline. This spirituality does not mean attending church if that is not your style. You will need to determine what a spiritual practice means to you, and then take care of your spirituality. Even taking a walk alone in the woods can be a spiritual experience. Through your spirituality, you will practice contentment, learning about yourself, surrendering to the divine, being happy with less, and cleanliness.

Next, you will learn the poses that make up the yoga part of the practice in the third limb. In your training, you will discover that your body is your temple and needs to be revered and cared for. The yoga poses will develop your ability to concentrate and your habit of discipline. The fourth limb is controlling your breath, where you will learn different techniques that will teach you how to manage your respiratory processes. You will also learn more about the connection between your emotions and your mind and breath. Proper breathing techniques will not only revive your body, but it will also help you live longer. The first four limbs of Ashtanga yoga deal mainly with you and your body. You will learn to develop an energetic awareness of yourself, gain mastery over your body, and refine your personality. All of this will help prepare you for the second part of your journey and the next four limbs that deal more with the use of your newly opened Third Eye.

When you begin the fifth limb of Ashtanga yoga, you will make a conscious effort to turn inward to your mind. You will draw your awareness away from stimuli from the outside and the wider world. You will direct your attention inward as you become more aware of your senses, even while you are removing your focus from them. You will need to take a few steps back and look at yourself honestly. This self-examination will also allow you to examine any cravings you might have and work to get rid of them since they will interfere with your spiritual growth and ruin your health.

The first five stages have prepared you for the sixth limb, the one of concentration. Now that you have removed the outside distractions from your life, you can begin to deal with all of the distractions inside your mind. Concentration comes before meditation, and it will allow you to slow down your thinking by focusing on a single object. This focus will be a purely mental focus, not on an actual item, and it can be the silent repetition of a sound, an image of the divine, or one of the energy centers in your own body. You have already started to withdraw from your senses by controlling your breathing and developing your ability to concentrate. Now you will focus on a single item and not allow your mind to wander during your practice. When you can focus for long periods of time, this will lead you naturally into meditation.

The seventh limb of Ashtanga yoga is the practice of meditation. This meditation is the uninterrupted flow of your concentration. You will notice a definite line of distinction between concentration and meditation, even though the two work together. Concentration involves focusing on a single thing, while meditation is more concerned with being acutely aware without focusing on any one thing. In this stage, your mind has learned to be quiet and produce few thoughts or none at all. It takes stamina and strength to get to this point. If you do not reach this point right away, keep trying. Yoga is not a goal, it is a practice, and you may need more time to achieve the results you want to achieve.

Once you have traveled through the first seven stages of Ashtanga yoga, you will be ready for the eight steps, the final limb, and the exalted state of ecstasy. When you reach this stage, you will be able to merge with the point you are focusing on and completely transcend yourself.

This will give you the connection to the divine you are seeking, and it will show you your connection to the entire Universe. This realization will give you the peace that will surpass all levels of conscious understanding. This aspiration is not a lofty goal or one that makes you better than other people. It is a goal that most people hope to obtain in life, the freedom and fulfillment of achieving their hopes and desires. The completion of the path is the goal of most people, and that goal is internal peace. This peace will give you the enlightenment you need to achieve your self-realization.

Your journey through the eight stages can sometimes be difficult, so be kind to yourself. Some may call this selfishness, but it is just taking care of you. You will not be able to achieve the enlightenment that comes with a functioning Third Eye is you are not prepared physically, mentally, and emotionally. Be honest about how you feel. The purpose of mental yoga is learning to put yourself first so that you are prepared for the demands of life.

## Spiritual Beings on Earth

When your Third Eye has awakened and you can receive and send messages with your mind, you will also find that you are more intuitive when it comes to an understanding of other people. This understanding will not only make you more empathetic, but it will allow you to see the spiritual side of other people. Since humans are spirits living in the astral plane known as earth, you will be able to discern the souls who are around you. Everyone who has gone on to another astral plane leaves a part of themselves behind, and you will recognize them through the powers of your Third eye.

Those who are reincarnated after they die will return to earth in another form, usually a human, The idea is that they will need to live again to satisfy some sort of karmic imbalance from their previous life. Sometimes only a part of the soul will come back to earth, and the rest of it will reside on another astral plane. A human spirit can be made up of as many as six parts, and it is not uncommon for the different parts to take turns returning to earth, while the others stay on the astral plane. When they come back together, they will compare experiences and prepare for the next incarnation. When the soul returns to earth, it will bring its spirit guardian. Sometimes that spirit guardian is one of the other parts of the soul from the astral plane.

The guardian spirit comes to earth with the human to watch over them and help protect them. They will also inspire their humans to make the right decisions. The guardian spirit can travel between the human world and the spirit world as they choose. The guardian wants their human to be safe, but also to be happy. You can receive guidance from your spirit guardian by simply acknowledging their presence in your world. When your Third Eye is open, it will be easier for you to receive guidance, and it will be more vital for you to seek advice from your spirit guardian. Opening your Third Eye can be stressful and scary, and your spirit guardian will be able to help you through the changes you will experience calmly. Your spirit guardian will come from one of many different sources.

Guardian angels belong only to you, and they will devote all of their time to taking care of you. They come with you when you are born, and they will leave when you die. The archangel is the leader angel of all of the spirit guides. These spirit guardians are loaded with powerful energy. When you call for assistance from an archangel, you will most likely feel an extra surge of life, especially if you are extra sensitive or you are empathic. Helper angels can help you at any time because they are not attached to anyone human. They work freely and go wherever they are most needed. Any of these spirit guardians can help you relieve the stress that comes from utilizing the power of your Third Eye.

Sometimes the people you have known and loved will come back to be your spirit guardian after they leave earth. Any human who has lived and died can become a spirit guardian, and they will generally seek someone who is similar to themselves in thought and action. If you are struggling with the perceptions from your Third Eye, call on one of these spirit guardians, especially seeking one who had their struggles with Third Eye enlightenment.

Your spirit guardian will not be able to contact you directly until you contact them first. They will send you messages, mainly through Third Eye reception, so you need to be open to receiving these messages. Sometimes they will come to you as feelings or thoughts, and sometimes they will come to you as concrete symbols of a message you are seeking. If you see a self-help book on a day you are feeling particularly needy spiritually or emotionally, then that might be a sign from your spirit guardian. They might send messages to you with numbers you consider to be lucky. They might make you think of a special person when you hear a particular song. Your spirit guardians have many ways to get messages to you, so you need to be receptive to your thoughts and the signs you see.

Methods that you can use to facilitate communication with your spirit guardian will also help you strengthen the powers of your Third Eye. Develop a regular spiritual practice. Send your spirit guardian a specific message. Experiment with divination by using oracle cards, runes, or tarot cards. Hold the item in your hands and ask for guidance from your spirit guardian before you begin. Give your spirit guardian a particular problem that you need help with, and then wait patiently for the answer.

Practice with different methods to improve your clairvoyance. Write about your spirit guardian in a journal. Give your spirit guardian a unique name that no one but you and they would know. And work on being mindful, so that you are mentally and emotionally present and available when your spirit guardian sends messages to you. Your physical eye will tell you everything that you need to know about the physical world, but your Third Eye will give you all the information you need about heavenly matters and your spirit guardian. When your Third Eye is open, you will be able to see beyond the restraints of the physical world, and you will understand your connection to the larger world.

## Earth Angels and Advanced Spirits

Some of the spirit guardians are real angels from Heaven who have come to help you. They have important things to do one earth. They will help you open your Third Eye and learn to use it for good purposes. They will help you realize your full potential once your Third Eye is open. Helping you raise your vibrational level so that you can freely send and receive messages through your Third Eye is one of their specialties. Their ultimate goal is to make your ability to communicate with the spirit world stronger.

Angels are compassionate beings who do not tolerate violence or anything that is not real. The Laws of the Universe guide them, and they operate on the principles of love, purity, and trust. Unfortunately, they believe that all people they encounter will feel the same way that they do, so they are often disappointed. If you meet an angel on earth, you will know it, for they are gentle souls who often resemble extensive children. The happiness they carry in their hearts keeps them looking perpetually young. They are unusually sensitive to the energies in the people around them and the vibration that people emit.

The advanced spirits will travel a difficult path while they are on earth. Their job here on earth is to restore harmony, love, and balance to humanity. The spiritual way they walk is one designed to improve the world by making people more in tune with their feelings and thoughts, and open to ideas from the spirit world. They connect with people in a completely selfless manner. All of the entities of the world are open to their guidance, whether that entity is human, animal, or plant. Even if their lives are not ideal, they will always seek their higher purpose in life, and they will work to help you find your higher purpose. They will never react to anyone or anything with anger or bitterness. Advanced spirits will spend all of their time trying to bring out the best in all people. Emanating a magnetic field that draws needy people to them, they have brightly shining lights that make them easy to find.

## The Third Eye and Your Aura

Having an open Third Eye will give you the ability to see the aura of other people. Since an aura is created from the colors that will correspond to the energies that come off the other person, reading their aura is almost like looking into their soul. All living people have their aura that surrounds them like a blanket, showing off their real personality to anyone who can read their aura. When your Third eye is open, you will be able to read auras with a little practice. Auras are made of seven separate layers, and each layer corresponds to one of the chakras inside of the person. The aura is the external reflection of the inner subtle body of the person. Those people who have more internal energy will have a more massive aura. Every aura has a unique pattern of blockages and openings that correspond to the internal energy of the person. Once you have developed your powers of clairvoyance, you will easily be able to read auras.

Each aura is made of three distinct planes and seven bodies of energy. The three planes are the physical plane, the spiritual plane, and the astral plane. The physical plane includes your etheric body, your emotional body, and your mental body. The physical plane and the spiritual plane are linked together by the astral plane. The spiritual plane works to connect you to your intuition and the divine. It is your spiritual plane that is the most crucial aspect of your spiritual self and your Third Eye. The different colors in your aura will directly reflect the health of the internal chakras in your body. If any of your chakras are not healthy, that will be displayed in the color and health of your aura. The differences in the colors of the aura will tell how you are feeling mentally, physically, emotionally, and spiritually. Your aura will continue to change colors as the health of your chakras changes. The aura is attached to you with thin attachment cords that hold it to your body. Besides the appearance of the colors, the aura can also show holes and tears if the chakra is damaged.

If you want to be able to read and understand the aura of someone accurately, then you will need to understand what the colors mean. You also need to know where your aura ends, and the aura of the other person starts so that you are not transferring information about your aura to the aura of the person that you are reading. When your Third Eye is well developed, you will easily read an aura by merely glancing at it. It will also help you know the strength of the personality and the spirit of the other person, and be able to tell where they might be suffering a blockage.

## Mirrors and Crystal Balls

Scrying is an essential method for divination for anyone who has opened their Third Eye. Mirrors and crystal balls are both used for scrying. Detecting messages of significance or visions is the primary purpose of scrying. You can use scrying for divination. You might be looking for some sort of personal guidance, prophecy, revelation, or inspiration when you are scrying. Crystallomancy, which is the method of using mirrors or crystal balls for scrying, is a form of spiritual work that you will take part in when your Third eye is open. You might want to keep your mirror or your crystal ball in a place of honor, such as on an altar.

When you do a reading, you are seeking to find a visionary sight that will provide you with knowledge about a particular subject. You can do a reading for yourself or someone else. Gazing into the mirror or the crystal ball will reveal psychic visions. Diviners and psychic readers who use mirrors or crystal balls for information will often study stones and crystals to learn more about their traditional knowledge. A stone or crystal can be used in place of a mirror or crystal ball when needed. Some readers will have different types of crystals for various purposes, their crystal ball being the largest one and the one that is most often used. If you choose to use crystals, then you will want to select the ones that have intentions and purposes that match your question. Quartz or calcite will be used when you want to send out blessings to someone, or if you need to see far into the distance either spiritually or physically. A piece of amethyst can let you know if someone is carrying addictions they want to keep hidden. Black obsidian would be used to determine if there is terrible magic working against someone.

Before you perform a reading, you will need to cleanse your mirror or crystal ball. Of course, you would keep it clean, but this type of cleansing has more to do with removing the remnants of past readings and any negative information the crystal ball has retained. You can use water, smoke, or herbs to clean your crystal ball. If you are using water to cleanse the ball, it should not be tap water, but some form of purified water. Rainwater is also a good choice for cleansing purposes. Add sea salt to the water and let the ball soak, fully immersed, for twenty-four hours, then wipe it with a clean white cloth. If you are using herbs, then you will want to smudge the ball. Put the herbs of your choice in a heatproof bowl and ignite them. Sandalwood, frankincense, and sage will work well for this purpose. When the herbs begin to give off smoke, use your hands to guide the smoke to waft over the crystal ball. Then wipe the ball with a clean white cloth. If there is a safe place in your yard, then you can bury the crystal ball for twenty-four hours and let the power of the earth cleanse it.

When you have cleansed your crystal ball, you are ready to perform the reading. If you need to clean the ball first, then do that one full day before the reading. You can perform a reading anywhere, but it is best done in a quiet place that is free of interruptions and distractions. Use herbs or incense to smudge the area where you will do the reading. Layout some crystals around the room to help protect your reading from unwanted intrusions of unrelated messages. Send out to the universe your intention to only invite positive messages and energies to participate in your reading.

Cradle the stone or ball gently in your hands. If you are using a large crystal ball, then you can place it in a holder on the table directly in front of you. When you are close to the sphere, you will make contact with it, and this is needed so that you can connect with its energies, so if you are not holding the crystal ball, then touch it with both hands. Breathe in and out deeply three times, repeating the word 'relax' as you exhale. Continue breathing while you focus on your breaths and let all of your thoughts disappear into the background. Gaze into the crystal ball and hold this gaze for several minutes. Let the messages and visions enter your mind through your Third Eye. Do not concentrate on them or try to force them to appear. You might see simple forms and shapes within the crystal ball, and scenes and images may appear in your mind. The divine may also send messages to you at this time. Depending on your ability and the level of trance you can reach, a reading can last anywhere from a few minutes to several hours.

When you have finished your reading, always remember to thank the divine energies for the wisdom they provided you in this session. Take three deep breaths to stabilize yourself. Come out of the trance slowly and allow your thoughts and energies to realign within you.

## The Afterlife and the Third Eye

When you have opened your Third Eye, and you are using its powers to amplify your life, you will be able to communicate with celestial beings and people who have died and left this physical world. When people die, their stream of consciousness, which makes up their energy, will continue to live on in an astral plane. This part of you might be your spirit or your soul, or it might just be a part of your essence that lives on after you are gone. With an open Third eye, you will be able to make contact with these souls and spirits in the astral plane. The eventual landing place of a departed soul will depend on their previous life on earth and their personal beliefs. They might spend eternity in their version of Heaven. They may be reincarnated back into the world. It is believed that those souls who are reincarnated will have no memory of the life they lived before so that you may encounter the same spirit in several different forms throughout your life.

Since everyone will eventually die, it is best to form your own opinion of it and learn to accept the inevitable. With your open Third Eye, you will be able to continue communicating with those who are gone, and with others after you are gone. Part of the fear of death is the absence of knowledge of what happens after you die. There are many theories around life after death, people have reported having near-death experiences, and some people will admit that they have lived before. There are reports of softness, lovely colors, and intensely bright lights that surround the end of the corridor where you are prompted to walk at the end of your life. It is possible that the passage does not lead to the end of your journey but is simply the doorway to the next trip. Christians hold that God does exist, and there is a Heaven, and this is where you want to go when you die. Buddhists do not believe that people have a soul, but they do think that everyone goes on into their new existence shortly after death. Since atheists do not believe in God or Heaven, they do not see this as the eventual destination. Some do believe in reincarnation and life on the astral plane after physical life is ended.

Reincarnation is also known as rebirth or transmigration, depending on the system of beliefs that you hold in your physical life. It is the philosophical or religious belief that your soul or spirit will take on a new life in a new physical form after the original physical body ceases to exist. When you take on your new way of life, the concept is that you will try to live a better life and be a better person than the one you had before. The new form that you take may depend on your behavior in your previous experience. Some people believe that if you were an undesirable person or live a less than desirable life in your last incarnation, then you will return as a less desirable life form in your next embodiment.

The idea behind reincarnation is to allow you to balance your karmic collections by living again when it is needed. As you go through life, you collect karmic impressions that are based on the kind of person you are and the kind of life you lead. People who try to do good things or live good lives will collect more positive karma than negative karma. A soul is not able to leave its physical body forever until its karmic balance is positive, so some people might go through many incarnations before they get the equation right. You will know who these people are on earth, through the power of intuition your Third Eye gives you, and you will be able to help them if you can. You can increase your positive karmic collection if you can help these people, and you do it with the correct intentions.

When a soul finally learns how to live the most moral incarnation they can live, when they bring their karmic balance to the positive, then they will be rewarded with salvation after their last death. For these souls, true salvation is the ability to stop being reborn, since being liberated from life is the real goal of reincarnation. This is the idea that the ancient teachers have handed down through the centuries. The modern view of reincarnation is that people come back because they want to, so they can complete something they failed to complete in their past life. They have indeed left unfinished business, but the souls do not come back of their own accord. They are told when to return to a new life. People believe in reincarnation to give them hope that life will go on after they leave the earth so that the next life does not seem so frightening. The idea of reincarnation gives you the chance to seek life after your current life has ended.

It is necessary to clear your karmic balance because you are not allowed to ascend to the astral plane until your karmic balance is on the positive side. There are many reasons for this. One of the most important reasons is that the inhabitants of the astral plane are the ones that people on earth seek guidance from. With your newly opened Third Eye, you have probably already sought advice from the inhabitants of the astral planes and other worlds. When you pursue this guidance, you want to know that it is coming from a reliable source and will be beneficial for you. This is why all of the souls that ascend to the astral plane will need to be pure and good.

Now that your Third Eye is open and functioning correctly, you can seek guidance and information from an infinite number of beings who have gone on before and who now inhabit the astral planes around you. These people are no further than a question away from you, and they now exist to help those on earth who need assistance gaining proficiency with their Third Eye and their new knowledge. As you are seeking information from the souls who have gone on before, you might encounter some beings that are at a higher level than most of the ascended beings you will encounter. These are the Ascended Masters who have finally moved beyond their physical incarnation and taken their rightful place in the astral world. These entities are more enlightened spiritually than most of the inhabitants of the astral plane, and they have fulfilled all of the physical incarnations they were required to perform. They will usually dwell in the highest dimension of the astral plane, the Fifth Dimension, but they are free to roam where they choose. As physical beings, they ascended to the rank of Healer, Shaman, Medicine Man, Master, Guru, or Yogi; they were people who were placed here with the ability to influence others. If you are lucky enough to know one of these people in their physical form, then know that you are in the presence of one who will become an Ascended Master after they die. They have learned all of the lessons that were set for them to know, they cleared their karmic slate, and they are ready to move on to their next divine plan.

Ascended Masters are the best teachers for anyone on earth who is struggling to adjust to their Third Eye and the power it brings. They work from the realm of the spirits to assist the spiritual needs of those on earth. They will inspire and motivate your spiritual growth and acceptance. They want you to succeed, particularly in matters involving the Third Eye and your new abilities. Call on them any time you are in need.

If you take the time to become used to the power your Third Eye will bring, then you will eventually be able to use it effortlessly. Your Third Eye is your window to other worlds and other people. Now that it is opened, take the time to develop your abilities because they will take you far in your life.

# CONCLUSION

Thank you for making it through to the end of *Kundalini*, let's hope it was interesting and informative and able to provide you with all of the tools you need to achieve your goals whatever they may be.

The next step is for you to begin your own journey toward spiritual enlightenment and astral awareness by taking the steps to awaken your Third Eye. This book has outlined the steps you can take and the methods that will help you as you move toward self-realization.

Awakening your Third Eye will give you the benefit of psychic powers that you can use to guide your life and make all things possible for you. It is easier to obtain the goals you have set for yourself when you have the wisdom and guidance of an infinite number or souls who have gone on before you. They are waiting on the astral plane, waiting to assist you with your psychic learning, but you will not be able to access their assistance until you awaken your Third Eye.

The path you walk will be uniquely yours, although others will be there to assist you. Use the information in this book to guide you along your path toward spiritual enlightenment and enrichment. You will not regret the choice.

Finally, if you found this book useful in any way, a review on Amazon is always appreciated!

# DESCRIPTION

Are many of your waking hours spent wondering if your life has any meaning? Do you look at other people and try to see them as they really are? Do you wonder if there are thoughts and ideas beyond the superficial ones that fill your mind each day? Has the possibility of other lives and other entities become more than a passing fantasy for you? If any of these ideas touch a spot in your soul, then you have come to the right place, because this is the book you need to answer all of your questions.

*Kundalini* is the quintessential guide to all things related to the Third Eye chakra and the powers it will bring to your life. It will explain everything that you need to know to awaken your Third Eye and utilize it to improve your experience.

The Third Eye chakra is the sixth internal chakra of the seven internal chakras and the one that is responsible for your powers of psychic vision and ability. This chakra allows you to increase the level of spiritual awareness in your daily life. You will be better able to navigate the world and all of its foibles when you expand your powers of intuition. You will then understand all of the capabilities available to you through

- Spirituality
- Channeling
- Mediumship
- Clairvoyance
- Mysticism
- Intuition

Increasing your awareness of spiritual matters is not difficult, and it is not out of the realm of possibilities for you. Everyone can tap into their psychic powers with a little practice, and that is what this book will show you how to do. It will instruct you in the methods that are used to awaken this chakra like

- Crystals
- Yoga
- Meditation
- Affirmations
- Essential oil
- Relaxing

Once you have awakened your Third Eye, you will have all the possibilities of the Universe at your disposal. You will be able to communicate with entities in other realms like the astral world. You will know about Ascended Masters to guide you on your spiritual path. You will know the truth that you seek in your daily life. You will have the power to cut through the drama and the illusion that clouds so much of your intuitive abilities, so that you can move on to an actual realization of your psychic powers.

And you will learn all of this and more when you buy this book, *Kundalini*. From the methods for awakening this chakra to the meaning of this chakra in your life, this book has all the information you need to begin your spiritual journey. From the history of the belief in the Third eye to its place in the modern world, all of the knowledge is right here, contained in these pages. Take this book and use it to lift your life to the exalted level you always knew was attainable. Once others around you see the new you, they will want this book too!